GOD?

POINT/COUNTERPOINT SERIES

Series Editor

James P. Sterba, University of Notre Dame

AFFIRMATIVE ACTION AND RACIAL PREFERENCE

Carl Cohen and James P. Sterba

GOD? A DEBATE BETWEEN A CHRISTIAN AND AN ATHEIST

William Lane Craig and Walter Sinnott-Armstrong

GOD?

A DEBATE BETWEEN A CHRISTIAN AND AN ATHEIST

William Lane Craig
Walter Sinnott-Armstrong

Point/Counterpoint Series
James P. Sterba, Series Editor

OXFORD
UNIVERSITY PRESS
2004

OXFORD
UNIVERSITY PRESS

Oxford   New York
Auckland   Bangkok   Buenos Aires   Cape Town   Chennai
Dar es Salaam   Delhi   Hong Kong   Istanbul   Karachi   Kolkata
Kuala Lumpur   Madrid   Melbourne   Mexico City   Mumbai
Nairobi   São Paulo   Shanghai   Taipei   Tokyo   Toronto

Published by Oxford University Press, Inc.
198 Madison Avenue, New York, New York, 10016
http://www.oup-usa.org

Oxford is a registered trademark of Oxford University Press

Library of Congress Cataloging-in-Publication Data
Craig, William Lane.
      God? : a debate between a Christian and an atheist / William Lane Craig,
Walter Sinnott-Armstrong.
          p.   cm.—(Point/counterpoint series)
                    ISBN 13 978-0-19-516600-2 (pbk. : alk. paper)

      1. God—Proof. 2. Atheism. I. Sinnott-Armstrong, Walter, 1955- II. Title. III.
      Point/counterpoint series (Oxford, England)
BT103.C73 2003
212′.1—dc21   2003042040

Printing number: 20 19 18 17 16 15 14 13 12 11 10

Printed in the United States of America
on acid-free paper

To Woody White—WLC

To Bill Kennick and Tracy Mehr—WS-A

CONTENTS

PREFACE

The question of whether or not God exists has been debated vigorously for millennia. It's easy to see why so many people remain intensely interested in this issue. According to traditional believers, human existence finds its ultimate fulfillment only in relation to God. Moreover, in the minds of many, eternal life hangs in the balance. The effects of belief or disbelief in God can also be dramatic in this world. Beliefs about God often influence positions on important and controversial issues, such as sexual behavior, abortion, medical research using stem cells, and, of course, prayer in public schools and government support for religious schools and charities. Many decisions in daily life—not just on Sunday—also depend on belief or disbelief in God. Social action has often been motivated by belief in God. Friendships, communities, and political alliances frequently form or break down because of common or conflicting beliefs about God. We all need to decide where we stand on the issue of God's existence.

Despite the antiquity of this question, new aspects of this debate have arisen recently, partly because of developments in science and philosophy. Big Bang cosmology is the best-known example, but each year brings new results of research into the origins of life and of our universe. Novel philosophical theories of causation, knowledge, and morality also bear on the arguments for and against the existence of God. Ongoing psychological research and the quest for the historical Jesus by biblical scholars also introduce relevant considerations. That is why these debates must be renewed continually.

Unfortunately, many debates about God overlook such recent developments and degenerate into simplistic rhetoric or mutual misunderstanding. Other discussions of God's existence become so technical that only experts can follow them. Neither of these extremes serves the needs of those who are sincerely concerned about whether or not to believe in God.

Our goal in this book is to steer a middle course between these extremes. We have formulated our positions in light of recent science and philosophy, but we have also avoided technical details that would be confusing or distracting to most readers. We try to focus on the arguments that are uppermost in the minds of non-specialists. For example, instead of investigating modal versions of the ontological argument, which even professional philosophers find obscure, we discuss religious experience, the Bible, evil, eternity, the origin of the universe, design, and the connection or lack of connection between morality and the existence of God. These considerations are what most people want to understand when they are deciding whether or not to believe in God.

We also try to avoid the mutual misunderstandings that plague debates about God. Many discussions get confused because theists defend non-traditional accounts of God that atheists do not deny or because atheists deny outmoded views about God that theists no longer defend. To avoid such misunderstandings, we agreed from the start that we were going to talk about God as He is usually defined within the Judaeo-Christian tradition. This ensures that what one of us claims is what the other denies. Moreover, our debate is not just about whether God can be known to exist. Agnostics deny that we can know that God exists, but agnostics do not deny that God exists. In contrast, Sinnott-Armstrong denies that God exists, whereas Craig claims that God exists. Our disagreement is not about the limits of knowledge but, instead, directly about whether God exists.

The style of our book results from its origin in live debates. Craig had already debated the existence of God with several philosophers around the United States, when he was invited to participate in another debate at Dartmouth College on November 4, 1999. Sinnott-Armstrong had never publicly debated or written on this topic, but he had expressed his views to students, one of whom asked him to face Craig. In that first debate, Craig argued for the existence of God, and then Sinnott-Armstrong criticized Craig's arguments and offered arguments to the contrary. The ensuing discussion was both fun and illuminating. The return match was held at Wooddale

Church in Eden Prairie, Minnesota on April 1, 2000. There Sinnott-Armstrong opened by arguing against the existence of God, and then Craig criticized Sinnott-Armstrong's arguments and offered arguments to the contrary. The extremely positive reactions to both of these debates were what made us decide to expand them into this book.

To retain the lively character of the debates, Craig developed his opening remarks at Dartmouth into Chapter 1 of this book, while Sinnott-Armstrong expanded his opening remarks in Minnesota into Chapter 4 of this book. After exchanging those chapters, Sinnott-Armstrong polished his criticisms at Dartmouth to produce Chapter 2 of this book, and Craig elaborated his remarks in Minnesota to create Chapter 5 of this book. Finally, after we exchanged Chapters 2 and 5, Craig wrote Chapter 3 in response to Sinnott-Armstrong's Chapter 2, and Sinnott-Armstrong constructed Chapter 6 as a reply to Craig's Chapter 5. Although we did later change a little wording and a few details in the chapters that were written earlier, we agreed not to change anything significant that would affect the other author's main criticisms in the chapters that were written later. Revisions and responses were saved for the closing chapters of each Part, Chapters 3 and 6. This order of composition means that, although each of us might prefer to make some changes in the chapters that were written earlier, our book as a whole should read more like an ongoing conversation where positions emerge and qualifications accumulate, much as they do in a live debate.

This origin in live debate also explains our conversational style. We do not pull our punches or go off on technical tangents. We give concrete examples and use common language. We are both aware that many details would need to be added if we were writing for an audience of professional philosophers of religion, but we chose to simplify our writing in order to increase our book's accessibility and liveliness.

We are also committed to fairness. That is why Craig gets to set the terms of the debate by going first, but Sinnott-Armstrong gets the last word. Also to ensure fairness, just as speakers are limited to the same time in real debates, we agreed to limit ourselves to approximately the same total number of words in each corresponding chapter. This plan forced us to make some of our points very concisely, but our brevity should enable our book to keep the attention of even the most impatient reader.

Or so we hope. Whether we succeed in these goals is, of course, for you to judge.

William Lane Craig would like to thank Craig Parker, who is a Campus Minister with the Navigators at Dartmouth College, *Voces Clamantium*, which is a Dartmouth student group that explores intellectual life from a Christian point of view, and the Cecil B. Day Foundation for their help in organizing and sponsoring our first debate. He also thanks Ken Geis, associate pastor at Wooddale Church in Eden Prairie, Minnesota, and Prof. David Clark of Bethel Seminary for arranging our second exchange. Finally, thanks are due, of course, to Walter Sinnott-Armstrong for being such a charitable and engaging partner, not only in each debate but also in the production of this book.

Walter Sinnott-Armstrong would also like to thank the sponsors of our two live debates, as well as William Lane Craig for providing such spirited and genial opposition. In addition, Sinnott-Armstrong is very grateful to all of his colleagues in various departments at Dartmouth College who helped him with details in their areas of expertise. These friends include, especially, Susan Ackerman, Rob Caldwell, Julia Driver, Bernie Gert, Marcelo Gleiser, Jack Hanson, Sam Levey, Laurie Snell, Christie Thomas, and James Walters, as well as many others whom he bothered with numerous questions on these issues over the years. He is also grateful to all of his students who encouraged him in this project, especially those who had the courage to stand up to him and argue against his views. In addition, a great debt is due to his magnificent research assistant, Kier Olsen DeVries, whose help in this project and many others has been simply outstanding. Finally, Sinnott-Armstrong would like thank Robert Miller at Oxford University Press for his support and encouragement, as well as the reviewers for the press, especially Ed Curley, for their detailed comments. Thanks to you all.

GOD?

PART 1

CHAPTER 1

Five Reasons God Exists

William Lane Craig

Does God exist? In order to answer that question rationally, we need to ask ourselves two further questions: (1) Are there good reasons to think that God exists? and (2) Are there good reasons to think that God does not exist?

Now with respect to the second question, I'll leave it up to Dr. Sinnott-Armstrong to present the reasons why he thinks that God does not exist, and then we can discuss them. For now I want to focus on the first question: What good reasons are there to think that God does exist?

I'm going to present five reasons why I think theism (the view that God exists) is more plausibly true than atheism (the view that He does not). Whole books have been written on each one of these reasons, so all I can present here is a brief sketch of each and then go into more detail as Dr. Sinnott-Armstrong responds to them.

As travelers along life's way, it's our goal to make sense of things, to try to understand the way the world is. The hypothesis that God exists makes sense out of a wide range of the facts of experience.

1. God Makes Sense of the Origin of the Universe

Have you ever asked yourself where the universe came from? Why everything exists instead of just nothing? Typically, atheists have said that the universe is just eternal, and that's all. But surely this is unreasonable. Just think about it a minute. If the universe never had a beginning, that means that the number of past events in the history of the universe is infinite. But mathematicians recognize that the existence of an actually infinite number of things leads to self-contradictions (unless you impose some wholly arbitrary rules to prevent this). For example, what is infinity minus infinity? Well, mathematically, you get self-contradictory answers. For example, if you subtract all the odd numbers {1, 3, 5, . . . } from all the natural numbers {0, 1, 2, 3, . . . }, how many numbers do you have left? An infinite number. So infinity minus infinity is infinity. But suppose instead you subtract all the numbers greater than 2—how many are left? Three. So infinity minus infinity is 3! It needs to be understood that in both these cases we have subtracted identical quantities from identical quantities and come up with contradictory answers. In fact, you can get any answer you want from zero to infinity!

This implies that infinity is just an idea in your mind, not something that exists in reality. David Hilbert, perhaps the greatest mathematician of the past century, states, "The infinite is nowhere to be found in reality. It neither exists in nature nor provides a legitimate basis for rational thought. . . . The role that remains for the infinite to play is solely that of an idea."[1] Therefore, since past events are not just ideas, but are real, the number of past events must be finite. Therefore, the series of past events can't go back forever; rather the universe must have begun to exist.

This conclusion has been confirmed by remarkable discoveries in astronomy and astrophysics. The astrophysical evidence indicates that the universe began to exist in a great explosion called the "Big Bang" around 15 billion years ago. Physical space and time were created in that event, as well as all the matter and energy in the universe. Therefore, as Cambridge astronomer Fred Hoyle points out, the Big Bang theory requires the creation of the universe from nothing. This is because, as one goes back in time, one reaches a point at which, in Hoyle's words, the universe was "shrunk down to nothing at all."[2] Thus, what the Big Bang model requires is that the universe began to exist and was created out of nothing.

Now this tends to be very awkward for the atheist. For as Anthony Kenny of Oxford University urges, "A proponent of the big bang theory, at least if he is an atheist, must believe that the . . . universe came from nothing and by nothing."[3] But surely that doesn't make sense! Out of nothing, nothing comes. In every other context atheists recognize this fact. The great skeptic David Hume wrote, "But allow me to tell you that I never asserted so absurd a Proposition as that *anything might arise without a cause.*"[4] The contemporary atheist philosopher Kai Nielsen gives this illustration: "Suppose you suddenly hear a loud bang . . . and you ask me, 'What made that bang?' and I reply, 'Nothing, it just happened.' You would not accept that. In fact you would find my reply quite unintelligible."[5] But what's true of the little bang must be true of the Big Bang as well! So why does the universe exist instead of just nothing? Where did it come from? There must have been a cause that brought the universe into being. As the eminent physicist Sir Arthur Eddington concluded, "The beginning seems to present insuperable difficulties unless we agree to look on it as frankly supernatural."[6]

We can summarize our argument thus far as follows:

1. Whatever begins to exist has a cause.
2. The universe began to exist.
3. Therefore, the universe has a cause.

Given the truth of the two premises, the conclusion necessarily follows.

Now from the very nature of the case, as the cause of space and time, this supernatural cause must be an uncaused, changeless, timeless, and immaterial being which created the universe. It must be uncaused because we've seen that there cannot be an infinite regress of causes. It must be timeless and therefore changeless—at least without the universe—because it created time. Because it also created space, it must transcend space as well and therefore be immaterial, not physical.

Moreover, I would argue, it must also be personal. For how else could a timeless cause give rise to a temporal effect like the universe? If the cause were a mechanically operating set of necessary and sufficient conditions, then the cause could never exist without the effect. For example, the cause of water's freezing is the temperature's being below 0° Centigrade. If the temperature were below 0° from eternity past, then any water that was around would be frozen from eternity. It would be impossible for the water to *begin* to freeze just a finite time ago. So if the cause is timelessly present, then the effect should be timelessly present as well. The only way for the cause to be timeless and the effect to begin in time is for the cause to be a personal agent who freely chooses to create an effect in time without any prior determining conditions. For example, a man sitting from eternity could freely will to stand up. Thus, we are brought, not merely to a transcendent cause of the universe, but to its personal Creator.

What objections might be raised against this argument? Premise (1) **Whatever begins to exist has a cause** seems obviously true—at the least, more so than its denial. Yet a number of atheists, in order to avoid the argument's conclusion, have denied the first premise. Sometimes it is said that sub-atomic physics furnishes an exception to premise (1), since on the sub-atomic level events are said to be uncaused. In the same way, certain theories of cosmic origins are interpreted as showing that the whole universe could have sprung into being out of the sub-atomic vacuum. Thus the universe is said to be the proverbial "free lunch."

This objection, however, is based on misunderstandings. In the first place, not all scientists agree that sub-atomic events are uncaused. Many physicists today are quite dissatisfied with this view (the so-called Copenhagen Interpretation) of sub-atomic physics and are exploring deterministic theories like those of David Bohm.[7] Thus, sub-atomic physics is not a proven exception to premise (1). Second, even on the traditional, indeterministic interpretation, particles do not come into being out of nothing. They arise as spontaneous fluctuations of the energy contained in the sub-atomic vacuum; they do not come from nothing.[8] Third, the same point can be made about theories of the origin of the universe out of a primordial vacuum.[9] Popular magazine articles touting such theories as getting "something from nothing" simply do not understand that the vacuum is not nothing, but is a sea of fluctuating energy endowed with a rich structure and subject to physical laws. Philosopher of science Robert Deltete accurately sums up the situation: "There is no basis in ordinary quantum theory for the claim that the universe itself is uncaused, much less for the claim that it sprang into being uncaused from literally nothing."[10]

So what about premise (2) **The universe began to exist**? The typical objection that is raised against the philosophical argument for the universe's beginning is that modern mathematical set theory proves that an actually infinite number of things can exist. For example, there are an actually infinite number of members in the set {0, 1, 2, 3, . . . }. Therefore, there's no problem in an actually infinite number of past events.

But this objection is far too quick. First, not all mathematicians agree that actual infinites exist even in the mathematical realm.[11] They regard series like 0, 1, 2, 3, . . . as merely *potentially* infinite; that is to say, such series approach infinity as a limit, but they never actually get there. Second, existence in the mathematical realm does not imply existence in the real world. To say that infinite sets exist is merely to postulate a realm of discourse, governed by certain axioms and rules that are simply presupposed, in which one can talk about such collections.[12] Given the axioms and rules, one can discourse consistently about infinite sets. But that's no guarantee that the axioms and rules are *true* or that an actually infinite number of things can exist in the *real* world. Third, in any case, the real existence of an actually infinite number of things would violate the rules of transfinite arithmetic. As we saw, trying to subtract infinite quantities leads to self-contradictions; therefore, transfinite arithmetic just prohibits such operations to preserve consistency. But in the real world there's nothing to keep us from breaking this arbitrary rule. If I had an actually infinite number of marbles, for example, I could subtract or divide them as I please—which leads to absurdity.

Sometimes it's said that we can find counter-examples to the claim that an actually infinite number of things cannot exist, so that this claim must be false. For instance, isn't every finite distance capable of being divided into 1/2, 1/4, 1/8, . . . , on to infinity? Doesn't that prove that there are in any finite distance an actually infinite number of parts? The fallacy of this objection is that it once again confuses a potential infinite with an actual infinite. You can continue to divide any distance for as long as you want, but such a series is merely potentially infinite, in that infinity serves as a limit that you endlessly approach but never reach. If you assume that any distance is *already* composed out of an actually infinite number of parts, then you're begging the question. You're assuming what the objector is supposed to prove, namely that there is a clear counter-example to the claim that an actually infinite number of things cannot exist.

As for the scientific confirmation of premise (2), it is true that there are alternative theories to the Big Bang theory that do not involve a beginning of the universe. But while such theories are possible, it has been the overwhelming verdict of the scientific community than none of them is more probable than the Big Bang theory. The devil is in the details, and once you get down to specifics you find that there is no mathematically consistent model that has been so successful in its predictions or as corroborated by the evidence as the traditional Big Bang theory. For example, some theories, like the Oscillating Universe (which expands and re-contracts forever) or the Chaotic Inflationary Universe (which continually spawns new universes), do have a potentially infinite future, but turn out to have only a finite past.[13] Vacuum Fluctuation Universe theories (which postulate an eternal vacuum out of which our universe is born) cannot explain why, if the vacuum was eternal, we do not observe an infinitely old universe.[14] The Quantum Gravity Universe theory propounded by the famous physicist Stephen Hawking, if interpreted realistically, still involves an absolute origin of the universe, even if the universe does not begin in a so-called singularity, as it does in the standard Big Bang theory.[15] In sum, according to Hawking, "Almost everyone now believes that the universe, and *time itself*, had a beginning at the Big Bang."[16]

In light of the evidence, both of the premises of the first argument thus seem more plausible than their denials. Hence, it is plausible that a transcendent Creator of the universe exists.

Some atheists have charged that the argument's conclusion is incoherent, since a cause must come before its effect, and there is no moment before the Big Bang. This objection, however, is easy to answer. Many causes and effects are simultaneous. Thus, the moment of God's causing the Big Bang just is the moment of the occurrence of the Big Bang. We can then say that God existing alone without the universe is either (i) before the Big Bang, not in physical time, but in an undifferentiated metaphysical time or else (ii) strictly timeless, but that He enters into time at the moment of creation. I am not aware of any incoherence in either of these alternatives.

Sometimes people will say, "But if the universe must have a cause, then what is God's cause?" But this question reveals an inattentiveness to the formulation of the argument. The first premise does not state **Whatever *exists* has a cause**, but rather **Whatever *begins to exist* has a cause**. The difference is important. The insight that lies at the root of premise (1) is that being cannot come from non-being, that something cannot come from nothing. God, since He never began to exist, would not require a cause, for He never came into being. Nor is this special pleading for God, since this is exactly what the atheist has always claimed about the universe: that it is eternal and uncaused. The problem is that the atheist's claim is now rendered untenable in light of the beginning of the universe.

In sum, we seem to have a good argument for God's existence based upon the origin of the universe.

2. God Makes Sense of the Fine-Tuning of the Universe for Intelligent Life

During the last 30 years or so, scientists have discovered that the existence of intelligent life like ours depends upon a complex and delicate balance of initial conditions given in the Big Bang itself. Scientists once believed that whatever the initial conditions of the universe were, eventually intelligent life might evolve. But we now know that our existence is balanced on a knife's edge. It seems vastly more probable that a life-*prohibiting* universe rather than a life-*permitting* universe like ours should exist. The existence of intelligent life depends upon a conspiracy of initial conditions that must be fine-tuned to a degree that is literally incomprehensible and incalculable. For example, Stephen Hawking has estimated that if the rate of the universe's expansion one second after the Big Bang had been smaller by even one part in a hundred thousand million million, the universe would have re-collapsed into a hot fireball.[17] British physicist P. C. W. Davies has calculated that in order to be suitable for later star formation (without which planets could not exist) the relevant initial conditions must be fine-tuned to a precision of one followed by a thousand billion billion zeroes, at least.[18] He also estimates that a change in the strength of gravity or of the weak force by only one part in 10^{100} would have prevented a life-permitting universe. Roger Penrose of Oxford University has calculated that the odds of the Big Bang's low entropy condition existing by chance are on the order of one out of $10^{10(123)}$.[19] There are around 50 such quantities and constants present in the Big Bang that must be fine-tuned in this way if the universe is to permit life. And it's not just *each* quantity that must be exquisitely finely-tuned; their *ratios* to one another must be also finely tuned. So improbability is added to improbability to improbability until our minds are reeling in incomprehensible numbers.

Now there are three possibilities for explaining the presence of this remarkable fine-tuning of the universe: natural law, chance, or design. The first alternative holds that the fine-tuning of the universe is physically necessary. There is some unknown Theory of Everything that would explain the way the universe is. It had to be that way, and there was really no chance or little chance of the universe's not being life-permitting. By contrast, the second alternative states that the fine-tuning is due entirely to chance. It's just an accident that the universe is life-permitting, and we're the lucky beneficiaries. The third alternative rejects both of these accounts in favor of an intelligent Mind behind the cosmos, who designed the universe to permit life. Which of these alternatives is the most plausible?

On the face of it, the first alternative seems extraordinarily implausible. It requires us to believe that a life-*prohibiting* universe is virtually physically *impossible*. But surely it does seem possible. If the matter and anti-matter had been differently proportioned, if the universe had expanded just a little more slowly, if the entropy of the universe were slightly greater, any of these adjustments and more would have prevented a life-permitting universe, yet all seem perfectly possible physically. The person who maintains that the universe must be life-permitting is taking a radical line, which requires strong proof. But there is none; this alternative is simply put forward as a bare possibility.

Moreover, there is good reason to reject this alternative. First, there are models of the universe that are different from the existing universe. As John Leslie explains, "The claim that blind necessity is involved—that universes whose laws or constants are slightly different aren't real physical possibilities . . . is eroded by the various physical theories, particularly theories of random symmetry breaking, which *show* how a varied ensemble of universes might be generated."[20] Second, even if the laws of nature were necessary, one would still have to supply initial conditions. As P. C. W. Davies states,

> Even if the laws of physics were unique, it doesn't follow that the physical universe itself is unique. . . . the laws of physics must be augmented

by cosmic initial conditions. . . . There is nothing in present ideas about 'laws of initial conditions' remotely to suggest that their consistency with the laws of physics would imply uniqueness. Far from it. . . .

. . . it seems, then, that the physical universe does not have to be the way it is: it could have been otherwise.[21]

The extraordinarily low entropy condition of the early universe would be a good example of an arbitrary quantity that seems to have just been put in at the creation as an initial condition. Thus, the first alternative is not very plausible.

What about the second alternative, that the fine-tuning of the universe is due to chance? The problem with this alternative is that the odds against the fine-tuning's occurring by accident are so incomprehensibly great that they cannot be reasonably faced. Students or laymen who blithely assert, "It could have happened by chance!" simply have no conception of the fantastic precision of the fine-tuning requisite for life. They would never embrace such a hypothesis in any other area of their lives—for example, in order to explain how, overnight, there came to be a car in their driveway.

But it's important to understand that it's not just the probability that's at stake here. After all, fantastically improbable events happen every day—your own existence, for example, is the result of an incredibly improbable union of a certain sperm and a certain egg, yet no one would infer that their union was therefore designed. Rather, what is at stake in eliminating the hypothesis of chance is what theorists call "specified probability": the demonstration that the event in question is not only improbable but also conforms to an independently discovered pattern.[22] Any sequence of letters hammered out by a chimpanzee seated at a typewriter is equally improbable; but if upon entering the room we find that a beautiful sonnet has been typed, then we know that this is not the result of blind chance, since it conforms to the independently given pattern of grammatical English sentences. In the same way, physics and biology tell us independently of any knowledge of the early conditions of the universe what the physical conditions requisite for life are. We then discover how incredibly improbable such conditions are. It is this combination of a specified pattern plus improbability that serves to render the chance hypothesis implausible.

With this in mind, we can immediately see the fallacy of those who say that the existence of any universe is equally improbable and therefore there is nothing here to be explained. It is not the improbability of some universe or other's existing that concerns us; rather it is the specified probability of a life-permitting universe's existing that is at issue. Thus, the proper analogy to the fine-tuning of the universe is not, as defenders of the chance hypothesis often suppose, a lottery in which any individual's winning is fantastically and equally improbable but which some individual has to win. Rather the analogy is a lottery in which a single white ball is mixed into a billion billion billion black balls, and you are asked to reach in and pull out a ball. Any ball you pick will be equally improbable; nevertheless, it is overwhelmingly more probable that whichever ball you pick, it will be black rather than white. Similarly, the existence of any particular universe is equally improbable; but it is incomprehensibly more probable that whichever universe exists, it will be life-prohibiting rather than life-permitting. It is the enormous, specified improbability of the fine-tuning that presents the hurdle for the chance hypothesis.

How can the atheist get over this hurdle? Some thinkers have argued that we really shouldn't be surprised at the finely tuned conditions of the universe, since if the universe were not fine-tuned, we wouldn't be here to be surprised about it! Given that we are here, we should expect the universe to be fine-tuned. But such reasoning is logically fallacious. The statement "We shouldn't be surprised that we do not observe conditions of the universe incompatible with our existence" is true. If the conditions of the universe were incompatible with our existence, we couldn't be here to observe them. So it's not surprising that we don't observe such conditions. But from that statement it does not logically follow that "We shouldn't be surprised that we *do* observe conditions of the universe which *are* compatible with our existence." Given the incredible improbability of such finely tuned conditions, it is surprising that we observe them.

Theorists who defend the alternative of chance have therefore been forced to adopt an extraordinary hypothesis: the Many Worlds Hypothesis. According to this hypothesis, our universe is but one member of a greater collection of universes, all of which are real, actually existing universes, not merely possible universes. In order to ensure that somewhere in the World Ensemble there will appear by chance a universe finely tuned for life, it is further stipulated that there are an infinite number of universes in the collection (so that every possibility will be realized) and that the physical constants and quantities are randomly ordered (so that the worlds are not all alike). Thus, somewhere in this World Ensemble there will appear by chance alone finely tuned universes like ours. We should not be surprised to observe finely tuned conditions, since observers like us exist only in those universes that are finely tuned.

Is the Many Worlds Hypothesis as plausible as the design hypothesis? It seems not. In the first place, it needs to be recognized that the Many Worlds Hypothesis is no more scientific, and no less metaphysical, than the hypothesis of a Cosmic Designer. As the scientist-theologian John Polkinghorne says, "People try to trick out a 'many universe' account in sort of pseudo-scientific terms, but that is pseudo-science. It is a metaphysical guess that there might be many universes with different laws and circumstances."[23] But as a metaphysical hypothesis, the Many Worlds Hypothesis is arguably inferior to the design hypothesis, because the design hypothesis is *simpler*. According to a principle known as Ockham's Razor, we should not multiply causes beyond what is necessary to explain the effect. But it is simpler to postulate one Cosmic Designer to explain our universe than to postulate the infinitely bloated collection of universes required by the Many Worlds Hypothesis. Only if there were a comparably simple mechanism for generating many worlds would the Many Worlds Hypothesis be as simple as theism. In the absence of such a mechanism, the design hypothesis is to be preferred.

Second, there is no known way for generating a World Ensemble. No one has been able to explain how or why such a collection of universes should exist. Moreover, those attempts that have been made require fine-tuning themselves. For example, although some cosmologists appeal to so-called inflationary theories of the universe to generate a World Ensemble, the only consistent inflationary model is Andrei Linde's Chaotic Inflationary Theory, and it requires fine-tuning to drive the inflation. As Robert Brandenburger of Brown University writes, "Linde's scenario does not address a crucial problem, namely the cosmological constant problem. The field which drives inflation in Linde's scenario is expected to generate an unacceptably large cosmological constant *which must be tuned to zero by hand*. This is a problem which plagues *all* inflationary universe models."[24]

Third, there is no evidence for the existence of a World Ensemble apart from the fine-tuning itself. The postulation of a World Ensemble thus represents an effort to multiply one's probabilistic resources without warrant just to increase the chances of obtaining the desired result. In the absence of independent evidence for a World Ensemble, the many-worlds theorizer is guilty of the Inverse Gambler's Fallacy (the attempt to render an event more probable by hypothesizing the existence of a previous series of unsuccessful throws of the dice). By contrast, not only is the hypothesis of a Cosmic Designer free of this fallacy, but it is again the better explanation because we do have independent evidence of the existence of such a Designer in the form of the other arguments for the existence of God.

Fourth, the Many Worlds Hypothesis faces a severe challenge from biological evolutionary theory.[25] First, a bit of background: During the nineteenth century, the German physicist Ludwig Boltzmann proposed a sort of Many Worlds Hypothesis to explain why we do not find the universe in a state of "heat death" or thermodynamic equilibrium, in which energy is evenly diffused throughout the universe.[26] Boltzmann hypothesized that the universe as a whole *does*, in fact, exist in an equilibrium state, but that over time fluctuations in the energy level occur here and there throughout the universe, so that by chance alone there will be isolated regions where disequilibrium exists. Boltzmann referred to these isolated regions as "worlds." We should not be surprised to see our world in a highly improbable disequilibrium state, since in the ensemble of all worlds there must exist by chance alone certain worlds in disequilibrium, and ours just happens to be one.

The problem with Boltzmann's daring Many Worlds Hypothesis was that if our world were merely a fluctuation in a sea of diffuse energy, then it is overwhelmingly more probable that we would be observing a much tinier region of disequilibrium than we do. In order for us to exist, a smaller fluctuation, even one that produced our world instantaneously by an enormous accident, is inestimably more probable than a progressive decline in entropy over billions of years to fashion the world we see. In fact, Boltzmann's hypothesis, if adopted, would force us to regard the past as illusory, everything having the mere appearance of age, and the stars and planets as illusory, mere "pictures" as it were, since that sort of world is vastly more probable, given a state of overall equilibrium, than a world with genuine temporally and spatially distant events. Therefore, Boltzmann's Many Worlds Hypothesis has been universally rejected by the scientific community, and the present disequilibrium is usually taken to be just a result of the initial low entropy condition mysteriously existing at the beginning of the universe.

Now a precisely parallel problem attends the Many Worlds Hypothesis as an explanation of fine-tuning. According to the prevailing theory of biological evolution, intelligent life like ourselves, if it evolves at all, will do so as late in the lifetime of the sun as possible. The less the time span available for the mechanisms of genetic mutation and natural selection to function, the lower the probability of intelligent life's evolving. Given the complexity of the human organism, it is overwhelmingly more probable that human beings will evolve late in the lifetime of the sun rather than early. In fact, Barrow and Tipler list ten steps in the evolution of human beings, *each of which* is so improbable that before it would occur the sun would have ceased to be a main sequence star and incinerated the Earth![27] Hence, if our universe is but one member of a World Ensemble, then it is overwhelmingly more probable that we should be observing a very old sun rather than a relatively young one of only a few billion years. If we are products of biological evolution, we should find ourselves in a world in which we evolve later in the lifetime of our star. In fact, adopting the Many Worlds Hypothesis to explain away fine-tuning also results in a strange sort of illusionism: it is far more probable that all our astronomical, geological, and biological estimates of age are wrong, that we really do exist very late in the lifetime of the sun and that the sun and the Earth's appearance of youth is a massive illusion.

Thus, the Many Worlds Hypothesis collapses and along with it the alternative of chance that it sought to rescue. Both the natural law alternative and the chance alternative are therefore implausible. We can summarize this second argument as follows:

1. The fine-tuning of the universe is due to either law, chance, or design.

2. It is not due to law or chance.
3. Therefore, it is due to design.

What objections might be raised to the alternative of design? According to this hypothesis there exists a Cosmic Designer who fine-tuned the initial conditions of the universe for intelligent life. Such a hypothesis supplies a personal explanation of the fine-tuning of the universe. Is this explanation implausible?

Detractors of design sometimes object that the Designer Himself remains unexplained. It is said that an intelligent Mind also exhibits complex order, so that if the universe needs an explanation, so does its Designer. If the Designer does not need an explanation, why think that the universe does?

This popular objection is based on a misconception of the nature of explanation. It is widely recognized that in order for an explanation to be the best, one needn't have an explanation of the explanation (indeed, such a requirement would generate an infinite regress, so that everything becomes inexplicable). If the best explanation of a disease is a previously unknown virus, doctors need not be able to explain the virus in order to know it caused the disease. If archaeologists determine that the best explanation of certain artifacts is a lost tribe of ancient people, we needn't be able to explain their origin in order to say justifiably that they produced the artifacts. If astronauts should find traces of intelligent life on some other planet, we need not be able to explain such extraterrestrials in order to recognize that they are the best explanation. In the same way, the design hypothesis's being the best explanation of the fine-tuning doesn't depend on our being able to explain the Designer.

Moreover, the complexity of a Mind is not really analogous to the complexity of the universe. A mind's *ideas* may be complex, but a mind itself is a remarkably simple thing, being an immaterial entity not composed of parts. Moreover, a mind in order to be a mind must have certain properties like intelligence, consciousness, and volition. These are not contingent properties that it might lack, but are essential to its nature. So it's difficult to see any analogy between the contingently complex universe and a mind. Detractors of design have evidently confused a mind's thoughts (which may be complex) with the mind itself (which is pretty simple). Postulating an uncreated Mind behind the cosmos is thus not at all like postulating an undesigned cosmos.

Thus, the design hypothesis does not share in the implausibility of its competitors and is a familiar sort of explanation that we employ every day. It is therefore the best explanation of the amazing fine-tuning of our universe.

3. God Makes Sense of Objective Moral Values in the World

If God does not exist, then objective moral values do not exist. When I speak of *objective* moral values, I mean moral values that are valid and binding whether anybody believes in them or not. Thus, to say, for example, that the Holocaust was objectively wrong is to say that it was wrong even though the Nazis who carried it out thought that it was right and that it would still have been wrong even if the Nazis had won World War II and succeeded in exterminating or brainwashing everyone who disagreed with them. Now if God does not exist, then moral values are not objective in this way.

Many theists and atheists alike concur on this point. For example, Bertrand Russell observed,

> . . . ethics arises from the pressures of the community on the individual. Man . . . does not always instinctively feel the desires which are useful to his herd. The herd, being anxious that the individual should act in its interests, has invented various devices for causing the individual's interest to be in harmony with that of the herd. One of these . . . is morality.[28]

Michael Ruse, a philosopher of science at the University of Guelph, agrees. He explains,

> Morality is a biological adaptation no less than are hands and feet and teeth. Considered as a rationally justifiable set of claims about an objective something, ethics is illusory. I appreciate that when somebody says 'Love thy neighbor as thyself,' they think they are referring above and beyond themselves. Nevertheless, such reference is truly without foundation. Morality is just an aid to survival and reproduction . . . and any deeper meaning is illusory.[29]

Friedrich Nietzsche, the great nineteenth century atheist who proclaimed the death of God, understood that the death of God meant the destruction of all meaning and value in life. I think that Friedrich Nietzsche was right.

But we must be very careful here. The question here is *not*: "Must we believe in God in order to live moral lives?" I'm not claiming that we must. Nor is the question: "Can we *recognize* objective moral values without believing in God?" I think that we can. Nor is the question: "Can we formulate an adequate system of ethics without reference to God?" So long as we assume that human beings have objective moral value, the atheist could probably draft a moral code that the theist would largely agree with.

Rather the question is: "If God does not exist, do objective moral values exist?" Like Russell and Ruse, I don't see any reason to think that in the absence of God, the herd morality evolved by *homo sapiens* is objective. After all, if there is no God, then what's so special about human beings? They're just accidental by-products of nature that have evolved relatively recently on an infinitesimal speck of dust lost somewhere in a hostile and mindless universe and that are doomed to perish individually and collectively in a relatively short time. On the atheistic view, some action, say, rape, may not be socially advantageous, and so in the course of human development has become taboo; but that does absolutely nothing to prove that rape is really wrong. On the atheistic view, there's nothing really *wrong* with your raping someone. Thus, without God there is no absolute right and wrong that imposes itself on our conscience.

But the problem is that objective values *do* exist, and deep down we all know it. There's no more reason to deny the objective reality of moral values than the objective reality of the physical world. As John Healey, the Executive Director of Amnesty International, wrote in a fund-raising letter, "I am writing you today because I think you share my profound belief that *there are indeed some moral absolutes*. When it comes to torture, to government-sanctioned murder, to 'disappearances'—there are no lesser evils. These are outrages against all of us."[30] Actions like rape, cruelty, and child abuse aren't just socially unacceptable behavior—they're moral abominations. Some things are really wrong. Similarly love, equality, and self-sacrifice are really good. But if moral values cannot exist without God and moral values do exist, then it follows logically and inescapably that God exists.

We can summarize this argument as follows:

1. If God does not exist, objective moral values do not exist.
2. Objective moral values do exist.
3. Therefore, God exists.

Again, let's consider possible objections that might be raised against this argument.

Some atheist philosophers, unwilling to bite the bullet and affirm that acts like rape or torturing a child are morally neutral actions, have tried to affirm objective moral values in the absence of God, thus in effect denying premise (1). Let's call this alternative Atheistic Moral Realism. Atheistic moral realists affirm that moral values and duties do exist in reality and are not dependent upon evolution or human opinion, but they insist that they are not grounded in God. Indeed, moral values have no further foundation. They just exist.

I must confess that this alternative strikes me as incomprehensible, an example of trying to have your cake and eat it, too. What does it mean to say, for example, that the moral value *Justice* simply exists? I don't know what this means. I understand what it is for a person to be just; but I draw a complete blank when it is said that, in the absence of any people, *Justice* itself exists. Moral values seem to exist as properties of persons, not as abstractions—or at any rate, I don't know what it is for a moral value to exist as an abstraction. Atheistic moral realists seem to lack any adequate foundation in reality for moral values, but just leave them floating in an unintelligible way.

Further, the nature of moral duty or obligation seems incompatible with Atheistic Moral Realism. Let's suppose for the sake of argument that moral values do exist independently of God. Suppose that values like *Mercy, Justice, Love, Forbearance*, and the like just exist. How does that result in any moral obligations for me? Why would I have a moral duty, say, to be merciful? Who or what lays such an obligation on me? As the ethicist Richard Taylor points out, "A duty is something that is owed. . . . But something can be owed only to some person or persons. There can be no such thing as duty in isolation. . . . "[31] God makes sense of moral obligation because His commands constitute for us our moral duties. Taylor writes, "Our moral obligations can . . . be understood as those that are imposed by God. . . . But what if this higher-than-human lawgiver is no longer taken into account? Does the concept of a moral obligation . . . still make sense? . . . the concept of moral obligation [is] unintelligible apart from the idea of God. The words remain but their meaning is gone."[32] As a non-theist, Taylor therefore thinks that we literally have no moral obligations, that there is no right or wrong. The Atheistic Moral Realist rightly finds this abhorrent, but, as Taylor clearly sees, on an atheistic view there simply is no ground for duty, even if moral values somehow exist.

Finally, it is fantastically improbable that just that sort of creature would emerge from the blind evolutionary process who corresponds to the abstractly existing realm of moral values.[33] This seems to be an utterly incredible coincidence, when you think about it. It is almost as though the moral realm *knew* that we were coming. It is far more plausible to regard both the natural realm and the moral realm as under the hegemony or authority of a divine Designer and Lawgiver than to think that these two entirely independent orders of reality just happened to mesh.

Thus it seems to me that Atheistic Moral Realism is not a plausible view, but is basically a halfway house for philosophers who don't have the stomach for the moral nihilism or meaninglessness that their own atheism implies.

What, then, about premise (2) **Objective moral values do exist**? Some people, as we have seen, deny that objective moral values exist. I agree with them that IF there is no God, then moral values are just the products of socio-biological evolution or expressions of personal taste. But I see no reason to think that that is in fact all that moral values are. Those who think so seem to commit the genetic fallacy, which is trying to invalidate something by showing how it *originated*. For example, a socialist who tried to refute your belief in democratic government by saying, "The only reason you believe in democracy is that you were raised in a democratic society!" would be guilty of the genetic fallacy. For even if it were true that your belief is totally the result of cultural conditioning, that does absolutely nothing to show that your belief is false (think of people who have been culturally conditioned to believe that the Earth is round!). The truth of an idea is not dependent upon how that idea originated. It's the same with moral values. If moral values are *dis-*

covered rather than *invented*, then our gradual and fallible apprehension of the moral realm no more undermines the objective reality of that realm than our gradual, fallible apprehension of the physical world undermines the objective reality of the physical realm. We know objective moral values exist because we clearly apprehend some of them. The best way to show this is simply to describe moral situations in which we clearly see right and wrong: torturing a child, incest, rape, ethnic cleansing, racism, witch burning, the Inquisition, and so forth. If someone really fails to see the objective moral truth about such matters, then he is simply morally handicapped, like a color-blind person who cannot tell the difference between red and green, and there's no reason to think that his impairment should make us call into question what we see clearly.

From the truth of the two premises the conclusion follows logically that (3) **Therefore, God exists**. Thus, God makes sense of ethics in a way that atheism really cannot. So in addition to the metaphysical and scientific arguments for God, we have a powerful moral argument for God.

4. God Makes Sense of the Life, Death, and Resurrection of Jesus

The historical person Jesus of Nazareth was a remarkable individual. New Testament critics have reached something of a consensus that the historical Jesus came on the scene with an unprecedented sense of divine authority, the authority to stand and speak in God's place. That's why the Jewish leadership instigated his crucifixion for the charge of blasphemy—in effect, for slandering God. He claimed that in himself the Kingdom of God had come, and as visible demonstrations of this fact he carried out a ministry of miracle-working and exorcisms. But the supreme confirmation of his claim was his resurrection from the dead. If Jesus did rise from the dead, then it would seem that we have a divine miracle on our hands and, thus, evidence for the existence of God.

Now in discussing this issue, I'm not going to treat the New Testament as an inspired and therefore inerrant book, but simply as a collection of ordinary Greek documents coming down to us from the first century. I'm not interested, therefore, in defending the infallibility of the gospels. Rather I'm interested in determining, first, what facts concerning the fate of Jesus of Nazareth can be credibly established on the basis of the evidence and, second, what is the best explanation of those facts.

So let's look at that first question. There are at least four facts about the fate of the historical Jesus that are widely accepted by New Testament historians today. It's worth emphasizing that I'm not talking just about conservative scholars, but about the broad mainstream of New Testament scholarship.

> FACT #1: *After his crucifixion Jesus was buried by Joseph of Arimathea in a tomb.*

This fact is highly significant because it means that the location of Jesus' tomb was known to Jew and Christian alike in Jerusalem. New Testament researchers have established the fact of Jesus' honorable burial on the basis of evidence such as the following:

1. Jesus' burial is attested in the very old information (ca. < AD 36), which was handed on by Paul in his first letter to the church in Corinth, Greece.

2. The burial story is independently attested in the very old source material used by Mark in writing his gospel.

3. Given the understandable hostility in the early Christian movement toward the Jewish leaders, Joseph of Arimathea, as a member of the Jewish high court that condemned Jesus, is unlikely to be a Christian invention.

4. The burial story is simple and lacks any signs of legendary development.

5. No other competing burial story exists.

For these and other reasons, the majority of New Testament critics concur that Jesus was in fact buried by Joseph of Arimathea in a tomb. According to the late John A. T. Robinson of Cambridge University, the burial of Jesus in the tomb is "one of the earliest and best-attested facts about Jesus."[34]

> FACT #2: *On the Sunday after the crucifixion, Jesus' tomb was found empty by a group of his women followers.*

Among the reasons that have led most scholars to this conclusion are the following:

1. In stating that Jesus "was buried and he was raised on the third day," the old information transmitted by Paul in I Cor.15 3–5 implies the empty tomb.

2. The empty tomb story is also multiply and independently attested in Mark, Matthew, and John's source material, some of which is very early.

3. The empty tomb story as related in Mark, our earliest account, is simple and lacks signs of legendary embellishment.

4. Given that the testimony of women was regarded as so unreliable that they were not even permitted to serve as witnesses in a Jewish court of law, the fact that it is women, rather than men, who are the chief witnesses to the empty tomb is best explained by the historical facticity of the narrative in this regard.

5. The earliest known Jewish response to the proclamation of Jesus' resurrection, namely, "The disciples came and stole away his body" (Matt. 28: 13–15), was itself an attempt to explain why the body was missing and thus presupposes the empty tomb.

One could go on, but I think enough has been said to indicate why, in the words of Jacob Kremer, an Austrian specialist on the resurrection, "By far most exegetes hold firmly to the reliability of the biblical statements concerning the empty tomb."[35]

> FACT #3: *On multiple occasions and under various circumstances, different individuals and groups of people experienced appearances of Jesus alive from the dead.*

This is a fact that is virtually universally acknowledged among New Testament scholars, for the following reasons:

1. Given its early date, as well as Paul's personal acquaintance with the people involved, the list of eyewitnesses to Jesus' resurrection appearances, quoted by Paul in I Cor. 15.5–8, guarantees that such appearances occurred.

2. The appearance narratives in the gospels provide multiple, independent attestation of the appearances.

Even the skeptical German New Testament critic Gerd Lüdemann therefore concludes, "It may be taken as historically certain that Peter and the disciples had experiences after Jesus' death in which Jesus appeared to them as the risen Christ."36

> *Finally,* FACT #4: *The original disciples suddenly and sincerely came to be-lieve that Jesus was risen from the dead despite their having every predis-position to the contrary.*

Think of the situation the disciples faced following Jesus' crucifixion:

1. Their leader was dead, and Jewish Messianic expectations in-cluded no idea of a Messiah who, instead of triumphing over Israel's enemies, would be shamefully executed by them as a criminal.

2. According to Old Testament law, Jesus' execution exposed him as a heretic, a man literally accursed by God.

3. Jewish beliefs about the afterlife precluded anyone's rising from the dead to glory and immortality before the general resurrection of the dead at the end of the world.

Nevertheless, the original disciples suddenly came to believe so strongly that God had raised Jesus from the dead that they were willing to die for the truth of that belief. Luke Johnson, a New Testament scholar at Emory University, states, "Some sort of powerful, transformative ex-perience is required to generate the sort of movement earliest Chris-tianity was."37 N. T. Wright, an eminent British scholar, concludes, "That is why, as a historian, I cannot explain the rise of early Chris-tianity unless Jesus rose again, leaving an empty tomb behind him."38

In summary, then, there are four facts concerning the fate of Jesus of Nazareth that are agreed upon by the majority of scholars who have written on this subject: Jesus' honorable burial by Joseph of Arimathea, the discovery of his empty tomb, his post-mortem ap-pearances, and the origin of the disciples' belief in his resurrection.

But that leads to our second concern: what is the best explanation of these facts? I think that the best explanation in this case is the one that was given by the eyewitnesses: God raised Jesus from the dead. In his book *Justifying Historical Descriptions*, historian C. B. McCullagh lists six tests that historians use in determining which is the best explanation for a given body of historical facts.39 The hy-pothesis "God raised Jesus from the dead" passes all these tests.

1. It has great *explanatory scope*. It explains why the tomb was found empty, why the disciples saw post-mortem appearances of Jesus, and why the Christian faith came into being.

2. It has great *explanatory power*. It explains why the body of Jesus was gone, why people repeatedly saw Jesus alive despite his earlier public execution, and so forth.

3. It is *plausible*. Given the historical context of Jesus' own unparalleled life and claims, the resurrection makes sense as the divine confirmation of those radical claims.

4. It is *not ad hoc* or *contrived*. It requires only one additional hypothesis: that God exists.

5. It is *in accord with accepted beliefs*. The hypothesis "God raised Jesus from the dead" does not in any way conflict with the accepted belief that people don't rise *naturally* from the dead. The Christian accepts *that* belief as wholeheartedly as he accepts the hypothesis that God raised Jesus from the dead.

6. It *far outstrips any of its rival theories* in meeting conditions 1–5. Down through history, various alternative explanations of the facts have been offered; for example, the conspiracy theory, the apparent death theory, the hallucination theory, and so forth. Such hypotheses have been almost universally rejected by contemporary scholarship. No naturalistic hypothesis has, in fact, attracted a great number of scholars. Thus, the best explanation of the established facts seems to be that God raised Jesus from the dead.

Thus, it seems to me that we have a good inductive argument for the existence of God based on the evidence for the resurrection of Jesus. It may be summarized as follows:

1. There are four established facts concerning the fate of Jesus of Nazareth: his honorable burial by Joseph of Arimathea, the discovery of his empty tomb, his post-mortem appearances, and the origin of his disciples' belief in his resurrection.
2. The hypothesis "God raised Jesus from the dead" is the best explanation of these facts.
3. The hypothesis "God raised Jesus from the dead" entails that God exists.
4. Therefore God exists.

5. God Can Be Immediately Known and Experienced

This isn't really an argument for God's existence; rather it's the claim that we can know that God exists wholly apart from arguments simply by immediately experiencing Him. This was the way people described in the Bible knew God, as Professor John Hick explains:

> God was known to them as a dynamic will interacting with their own wills, a sheer given reality, as inescapably to be reckoned with as destructive storm and life-giving sunshine. . . . They did not think of God as an inferred entity but as an experienced reality. . . . To them God was not a proposition completing a syllogism, or an idea adopted by the mind, but the experiential reality which gave significance to their lives.[40]

For these people, God was not inferred to be the best explanation of their religious experience and so they believed in Him; rather in their religious experience they came to know God *directly*.

Philosophers call beliefs like this "properly basic beliefs." They aren't based on some other beliefs; rather they are part of the foundation of a person's system of beliefs. Other properly basic beliefs would be the belief in the reality of the past, the existence of the external world, and the presence of other minds like your own. When you think about it, none of these beliefs can be proved. How could you prove that the world was not created five minutes ago with built-in appearances of age, such as food in our stomachs from the breakfasts we never really ate and memory traces in our brains of events we never really experienced? How could you prove that you are not a brain in a vat of chemicals being stimulated with electrodes by some mad scientist and made to believe that you are now reading this book? How could you prove that other people are not really automata who exhibit all the external behavior of persons with minds, when in reality they are soulless, robot-like entities?

Although these sorts of beliefs are basic for us, that doesn't mean that they're arbitrary. Rather they are grounded, in the sense that they're formed in the context of certain experiences. In the experiential context of seeing and feeling and hearing things, I naturally form the belief that there are certain physical objects that I am sensing. Thus, my basic beliefs are not arbitrary, but appropriately grounded in experience. There may be no way to prove such beliefs, and yet it is perfectly rational to hold them. You would have to be crazy to think that the world was created five minutes ago or to believe that you are a brain in a vat! Such beliefs are thus not merely basic, but *properly* basic.

In the same way, belief in God is for those who seek Him a properly basic belief grounded in our experience of God, as we discern Him in nature, conscience, and other means. Now, someone might object that atheists or adherents to some non-personal religious faith like Taoism could also claim to know their beliefs in a properly basic way. Certainly, they could *claim* such a thing; but what does that prove? Imagine that you were locked in a room with four color-blind people, all of whom claimed that there is no difference between red and green. Suppose you tried to convince them by showing them red and green objects and asking, "Can't you *see* the difference?" Of course, they would see no difference at all and would dismiss your claim to see different colors as delusory. In terms of *showing* who's right, there would be a complete stand-off. But would their denial of the difference between red and green or your inability to show them that you are right do anything logically either to render your belief false or to invalidate your experience? Obviously not!

In the same way, the person who has actually come to know God as a living reality in his life can know with assurance that his experience is no delusion, regardless of what the atheist or Taoist tells him. In a recent discussion,[41] philosopher William Alston points out that in such a situation neither party knows how to demonstrate to the other that he alone has a veridical, rather than delusory, experience. But this stand-off does not undermine the rationality of belief in God, for *even if the believer's process of forming his belief were as reliable as can be*, he'd still have no way of giving a non-circular proof of this fact. Thus, the believer's inability to provide such a proof does not nullify the rationality of his belief. Still, it remains the case that in such a situation, although the believer may *know* that his belief is true, both parties are at a complete loss to *show* the truth of their respective beliefs to the other party. How is one to break this deadlock? Alston answers that the believer should do whatever is feasible to find common ground, using logic and empirical facts, by means of which he can show in a non-circular way whose view is correct. That is exactly the procedure that I have sought to follow in this chapter. I know that God exists in a properly basic way, and I've tried to show that God exists by appeal to the common facts of science, ethics, history, and philosophy.

Now if, through experiencing God, we can know in a properly basic way that God exists, then there's a real danger that proofs for God could actually distract one's attention from God Himself. If you're sincerely seeking God, God will make His existence evident to you. The Bible promises, "Draw near to God and He will draw near to you" (James 4.8). We mustn't so concentrate on the proofs for God that we fail to hear the inner voice of God speaking to our own heart. For those who listen, God becomes an immediate reality in their lives.

In summary, we've seen five good reasons to think that God exists:

1. God makes sense of the origin of the universe.
2. God makes sense of the fine-tuning of the universe for intelligent life.
3. God makes sense of objective moral values in the world.
4. God makes sense of the life, death, and resurrection of Jesus.
5. God can be immediately known and experienced.

These are only a part of the evidence for God's existence. Alvin Plantinga, one of America's leading philosophers, has laid out two dozen or so arguments for God's existence.[42] Together these constitute a powerful cumulative case for the existence of God. Unless and until we're given better arguments for atheism, I think that theism is the more plausible world view.

Notes

1. David Hilbert, "On the Infinite," in *Philosophy of Mathematics*, ed. with an Introduction by Paul Benacerraf and Hillary Putnam (Englewood Cliffs, N.J.: Prentice-Hall, 1964), 139, 141.

2. Fred Hoyle, *Astronomy and Cosmology* (San Francisco: W.H. Freeman, 1975), 658.

3. Anthony Kenny, *The Five Ways: St. Thomas Aquinas' Proofs of God's Existence* (New York: Schocken Books, 1969), 66.

4. David Hume to John Stewart, February 1754, in *The Letters of David Hume*, 2 vols., ed. J. Y. T. Greig (Oxford: Clarendon Press, 1932), 187.

5. Kai Nielsen, *Reason and Practice* (New York: Harper & Row, 1971), 48.

6. Arthur Eddington, *The Expanding Universe* (New York: Macmillan, 1933), 124.

7. See James T. Cushing, Arthur Fine, and Sheldon Goldstein, *Bohmian Mechanics and Quantum Theory: An Appraisal* in Boston Studies in the Philosophy of Science 184 (Dordrecht: Kluwer Academic Publishers, 1996).

8. See John Barrow and Frank Tipler, *The Anthropic Cosmological Principle* (Oxford: Clarendon Press, 1986), 441.

9. See Bernulf Kanitscheider, "Does Physical Cosmology Transcend the Limits of Naturalistic Reasoning?" in *Studies on Mario Bunge's "Treatise,"* ed. P. Weingartner and G. J. W. Dorn (Amsterdam: Rodopi, 1990), 346–347.

10. Robert Deltete, Critical notice of *Theism, Atheism, and Big Bang Cosmology*, by William Lane Craig and Quentin Smith, *Zygon* 30 (1995): 656. (N.B. the review was attributed to J. Leslie due to an editorial mistake at *Zygon*.)

11. See, for example, Abraham Robinson, "Metamathematical Problems," *Journal of Symbolic Logic* 38 (1973): 500–516.

12. See Alexander Abian, *The Theory of Sets and Transfinite Arithmetic* (Philadelphia: W. B. Saunders, 1965), 68; B. Rotman and G. T. Kneebone, *The Theory of Sets and Transfinite Numbers* (London: Oldbourne, 1966), 61.

13. See I. D. Novikov and Ya. B. Zeldovich, "Physical Processes near Cosmological Singularities," *Annual Review of Astronomy and Astrophysics* 11 (1973): 401–402; A. Borde and A. Vilenkin, "Eternal Inflation and the Initial Singularity," *Physical Review Letters* 72 (1994): 3305, 3307.

14. Christopher Isham, "Creation of the Universe as a Quantum Process," in *Physics, Philosophy and Theology: A Common Quest for Understanding*, ed. R. J. Russell, W. R. Stoeger, and G. V. Coyne (Vatican City: Vatican Observatory, 1988), 385–387.

15. See John D. Barrow, *Theories of Everything* (Oxford: Clarendon Press, 1991), 67–68.

16. Stephen Hawking and Roger Penrose, *The Nature of Space and Time*, The Isaac Newton Institute Series of Lectures (Princeton, N.J.: Princeton University Press, 1996), 20.

17. Stephen W. Hawking, *A Brief History of Time* (New York: Bantam Books, 1988), 123.

18. P. C. W. Davies, *Other Worlds* (London: Dent, 1980), 160–161, 168–169.

19. P. C. W. Davies, "The Anthropic Principle," in *Particle and Nuclear Physics* 10 (1983): 28.

20. John Leslie, *Universes* (London: Routledge, 1989), 202.

21. Paul Davies, *The Mind of God* (New York: Simon & Schuster, 1992), 169.

22. See William A. Dembski, *The Design Inference: Eliminating Chance through Small Probabilities*, Cambridge Studies in Probability, Induction, and Decision Theory (Cambridge: Cambridge University Press, 1998), 167–174.

23. John C. Polkinghorne, *Serious Talk: Science and Religion in Dialogue* (London: SCM Press, 1996), 6.

24. Robert Brandenburger, personal communication.

25. I owe this insight to the philosopher of science Robin Collins.

26. Ludwig Boltzmann, *Lectures on Gas Theory*, trans. Stephen G. Brush (Berkeley: University of California Press, 1964), 446–448.

27. Barrow and Tipler, *Anthropic Cosmological Principle*, 561–565.

28. Bertrand Russell, *Human Society in Ethics and Politics* (New York: Simon and Schuster, 1955), 124.

29. Michael Ruse, "Evolutionary Theory and Christian Ethics," in *The Darwinian Paradigm* (London: Routledge, 1989), 262–269.

30. John Healey, Amnesty International fund-raising letter, 1991.

31. Richard Taylor, *Ethics, Faith, and Reason* (Englewood Cliffs, N.J.: Prentice-Hall, 1985), 83.

32. Ibid., pp. 83–84.

33. See Gregory E. Ganssle, "Necessary Moral Truths and the Need for Explanation," *Philosophia Christi* 2 (2000): 105–112.

34. John A. T. Robinson, *The Human Face of God* (Philadelphia: Westminster, 1973), 131.

35. Jacob Kremer, *Die Osterevangelien—Geschichten um Geschichte* (Stuttgart: Katholisches Bibelwerk, 1977), 49–50.

36. Gerd Lüdemann, *What Really Happened to Jesus?* trans. John Bowden (Louisville, Ky.: Westminster John Knox Press, 1995), 8.

37. Luke Timothy Johnson, *The Real Jesus* (San Francisco: Harper San Francisco, 1996), 136.

38. N. T. Wright, "The New Unimproved Jesus," *Christianity Today* (September 13, 1993), 26.

39. C. Behan McCullagh, *Justifying Historical Descriptions* (Cambridge: Cambridge University Press, 1984), 19.

40. John Hick, Introduction, in *The Existence of God*, ed. with an Introduction by John Hick, Problems of Philosophy Series (New York: Macmillan, 1964), 13–14.

41. William Alston, "Religious Diversity and Perceptual Knowledge of God," *Faith and Philosophy* 5 (1988): 433–448.

42. Alvin Plantinga, "Two Dozen (or so) Theistic Arguments." Lecture presented at the 33rd Annual Philosophy Conference, Wheaton College, Wheaton, Illinois, October 23–25, 1986.

CHAPTER 2

There Is No Good Reason
to Believe in God

Walter Sinnott-Armstrong

In arguing for the existence of God, Craig uses a shotgun strategy. He shoots lots of arguments hoping that one will hit his target. This tactic has rhetorical advantages. A critic must try to block or dodge every argument. If the critic overlooks a single one, Craig can claim that it is a killer. Also, since there are so many arguments, a critic with limited space cannot build an impenetrable defense against any argument. Such is my predicament. I will try to refute Craig's main arguments, but I am bound to miss some lesser points, and my criticisms must be too brief.

The task of covering so many arguments can be reduced by mentioning three fallacies that recur. First, it is crucial to specify what an argument is supposed to prove. Here we agreed to debate the existence of a traditional Christian God, who is:

- All-good (= always does the best that He[1] can)
- All-powerful (= can do anything that is logically possible)
- All-knowing (= knows everything that is true)
- Eternal (= exists outside of time)
- Effective (= causes changes in time)
- Personal (= has a will and makes choices)

Craig's arguments do not focus on these features. What he argues for is a creator or a designer or an external source of religious experience. Then he adds, "and this is God." That conclusion does not follow. Even if there were a creator or designer or an external source of religious experience, it might not be all-powerful or all-good, or eternal. Consequently, it is a mistake to inflate a claim about a creator, designer, or cause of experience into a conclusion about God. This is the fallacy of *bloated conclusions*.

Second, many of Craig's arguments attack competing views. This is usually easy, since there are problems for any position in this area. However, showing that some competitors are false does not establish that God exists unless these are the only possibilities. They never are. In particular, it is a mistake to assume that either Jesus rose from the dead or his tomb was not empty, that either God caused the Big Bang or nothing did, and that either God forbids rape or rape is not immoral. In each case, additional alternatives are available, so an argument against one alternative gives no support to the other. To overlook extra possibilities is the fallacy of *false dichotomy*.

Third, Craig cites many authorities: Hawking, Healy, Hick, Hilbert, Hoyle, and Hume, just in the Hs. Watch out for authorities, especially when someone cites too many. This is the fallacy of *excessive footnotes*. It's fine to cite some authorities, but they must be cited accurately, in context, and on topics on which they really are authorities. Moreover, authorities have biases. Craig claims that most New Testament scholars believe that Jesus' tomb was empty. (23) Maybe so, but this should come as no surprise, since most people do not spend their lives studying the New Testament unless they accept Christianity to begin with. Most importantly, authorities are useless where controversy lives, as in philosophy. For every philosopher whom Craig cites, I could quote others who claim the opposite. Almost no view is so absurd that you can't find some philosopher who held it. But the fact that a philosopher says something is no argument that what that philosopher says is true. That goes for me, too. You have to judge for yourself.

[margin handwritten note: He has a point]

1. Morality

One example of a questionable appeal to authority occurs in Craig's argument from objective morality. Craig quotes Russell, Ruse, and Nietzsche, saying that there could not be objective values without God. Then he claims that there are objective values. He concludes that God exists.

It is important to get this argument out of the way right at the start, because it leads many religious believers to think that all atheists are immoral and dangerous. This is false. Many atheists are nice (including me, I hope). Craig admits this, but then he writes, "On the atheistic view, there's nothing really *wrong* with your raping someone." (18) Such misleading and inaccurate allegations inhibit mutual understanding.

In fact, many atheists are happy to embrace objective moral values. I agree with them. Rape is morally wrong. So is discrimination against gays and lesbians. Even if somebody or some group *thinks* that these acts are not morally wrong, they still *are* morally wrong, so their immorality is objective by Craig's own definition (17). Craig and I might not always agree about what is objectively morally wrong, but we do agree that some acts are objectively morally wrong.

This admission implies nothing about God, unless objective values depend on God. Why should we believe that they do? Because Russell, Ruse, and Nietzsche say so? But their claims are denied by many philosophers, atheists as well as theists. Even Russell and Ruse themselves denied these claims at other times in their careers. So Craig needs a reason to believe some authorities rather than others.

Craig does give some reasons to back up his authorities. One is that atheists see morality as a biological adaptation, but moral values are not objective if they depend on our biology. This argument commits a fallacy of *equivocation.* When anthropologists talk about a culture's morality, they describe a group of beliefs about what is right and wrong or good and bad. In contrast, when philosophers present a moral system, they seek a set of rules or principles that prescribes what really *is* morally right and wrong or good and bad. Morality in the philosophical sense can be objective, even if people's beliefs about it are subjective. After all, scientific beliefs have biological and cultural origins as well. Just as it is objectively true that the earth moves around the sun, although biology and culture lead some people to believe otherwise, so rape is objectively morally wrong, although biology and culture lead some people to believe otherwise. At least this position is not excluded by the biological and cultural origins of moral beliefs, so atheists can recognize those origins and still consistently believe in objective values.

Craig next asks, "If God did not forbid rape, what makes rape immoral objectively?" This question is supposed to be hard for atheists to answer, because Craig seems to assume that on "the atheistic view" (which one?) what makes rape wrong is some cost to the rapist or to society. (18) These views are inadequate because rape would still be immoral even if the rapist got away with it and even if society was not harmed. But atheists can give a better answer: What makes rape immoral is that rape harms *the victim* in terrible ways. The victim feels pain, loses freedom, is subordinated, and so on. These harms are not justified by any benefits to anyone. Craig still might ask, "What's immoral about causing serious harms to other people without justification?" But now it seems natural to answer, "It simply is. Objectively. Don't you agree?"

This simple answer implies nothing like "in the absence of any people, *Justice* itself exists," so atheists can agree with Craig that they "don't know what this means." (19) Atheists can also agree with Craig and Taylor that "A duty is something that is owed. . . . But something can be owed only to some person or persons." (19) The duty not to rape is owed to the victim. Thus, Craig's criticisms of "Atheistic Moral Realism" attack a *straw man*.

Craig suggests a deeper problem when he asks, "what's so special about human beings?" (18) If harm to the victim is what makes rape immoral, why isn't it also immoral when a lion causes harm by having forced sex with another lion? Atheists can answer that lower animals, such as lions, are not moral agents. They do not make free choices. Their actions are not determined by any conception of what is moral or not. That explains why moral rules and principles do not apply to lower animals any more than they apply to avalanches that kill people. You don't need to add that humans were made in God's image or that we are His favorite species or anything religious.

Philosophers still might long for deeper explanations of why it is immoral for moral agents to cause unjustified harm. Many atheists offer various explanations, but I do not want to commit myself to any particular account here. And I don't need to. Even if atheists were stuck with saying, "It *just is* immoral," that would be a problem for atheism only if theists could give a better answer. They cannot.

In the end, Craig himself says, "If someone really fails to see the objective moral truth about [rape], then he is simply morally handicapped." (21) This is no better (or worse) than saying, "Rape just is morally wrong."

Theists might give deeper accounts of morality, but atheists can adopt or adapt the same accounts—with only one exception. The only theory of morality that atheists cannot accept is one that refers to God, such as when theists claim that what makes rape immoral is that God commands us not to rape. This view faces a difficult question: Why should we obey God's commands? The answer cannot be that God will punish us if we disobey, since might does not make right. Even if a government commands you to turn in runaway slaves and will punish you if you don't, that does not make it morally wrong to hide runaway slaves. Some theists answer that we should obey God's commands because God gave us life. But our parents also gave us life, and yet, at least in modern societies, we do not have to marry whomever our parents tell us to. Theists might answer that it is simply immoral to disobey God, but that claim is no more illuminating than when atheists say that it is simply immoral to cause unjustified harm. A better answer is that God has good reasons for his commands. God commands us not to rape because rape harms the victim. But then that harm (not the command) is what makes rape immoral. Rape would be just as harmful without God, so rape would be morally wrong without God. To think otherwise is like a boy imagining that, once his parents leave, he may beat up his little sister, because the only thing that makes it wrong for him to beat up his sister is that his parents told him not to.

This basic point was presented long ago as a dilemma in Plato's dialogue, *The Euthyphro*: Is rape immoral because God commanded us not to rape or did God command us not to rape because rape is immoral? If God forbids rape because it is immoral, rape must be immoral prior to His command, so His command is not necessary to make it immoral. On the other hand, if God forbids rape but not because it is already immoral, God could have failed to forbid rape, and then there would be nothing immoral about raping whenever we want. That implication is unacceptable. Theists often respond that God cannot fail to command us not to rape, because He is good, and rape is bad. That response brings us right back to the first horn of the dilemma. If God's nature ensures that He will forbid rape because of how bad rape is, then God's command is not needed to make rape wrong. Rape is immoral anyway, and God is superfluous, except maybe for punishment or as a conduit of information.

This dilemma arises not only for rape but for all kinds of immorality. God's commands are arbitrary if He has no reason to command one act rather than another; but, if He does have reasons for His commands, then His *reasons* rather than His *commands* are what make acts immoral. Divine command theorists think that they can solve this dilemma, but all of their solutions fail, in my opinion. Anyway, I don't need to claim that much here. My current task is only to refute Craig's argument, so all I need to show is that atheists can coherently believe in an objective morality. They can, and I do.

2. Miracles

Craig's other arguments do not refer to morality. The next one refers to the resurrection of Jesus. If that resurrection occurred, it would be a miracle.

Some atheists try to prove the impossibility of miracles. One attempt defines a miracle as a violation of a law of nature and defines a law of nature as a generalization without any exception. Then, if Jesus walked on water, this act would be an exception to generalizations about buoyancy that we took to be laws of nature, so those generalizations would not really be laws of nature, and Jesus' walk on water would not really be a miracle. This is a cheap verbal trick. If anyone walks on water without any natural explanation, that is a miracle in my book. Such miracles are *logically possible*. I agree with Craig about this.

It is still a big step to the claim that we have *adequate evidence* to believe in any miracle. When people declare that a miracle occurred, we need to look at the evidence for and against their claims. The evidence *against* the miracle includes all of the evidence for the generalization that the miracle violates. Our common generalizations about buoyancy are supported by copious observations, plentiful testimony, numerous experiments, abundant explanations, and ample theories. To outweigh so much evidence, one would need a very strong reason to believe in any miracle.

I doubt that this burden is carried for any alleged miracle, but here I will focus on Craig's claims about the resurrection of Jesus. What is Craig's evidence for this miracle? First, "Jesus' tomb was found empty by a group of his women followers." (22) Unfortunately, our records come from years later. Craig describes the Gospels as "very early" and cites a date "ca. < AD 36." (22) The scholars whom I consulted suggested that dates > AD 50 are more likely. In any case, Craig's own dates imply years after Jesus' death, which is plenty of time for distortions to spread. The supposed witnesses were surely prompted often in the intervening years. They were likely subjected to tremendous social pressures. Their emotions undoubtedly ran high. They probably had neither the training nor the opportunity nor the inclination to do a careful, impartial investigation. Most people at that time were gullible, as shown by the plethora of cults. These are exactly the kinds of factors that psychologists have found to distort memory and eyewitness testimony in many cases. We would and should heavily discount witnesses like these in legal trials.

To defend his sources, Craig suggests that Jesus' followers had no expectation that Jesus would rise from the dead. (24) Witnesses *with* expectations are less reliable, but this does not show that witnesses *without* expectations *are* reliable. Moreover, we can't know that Craig's supposed witnesses had no expectations. Narratives like the story of Jesus' resurrection were common in that area around that time. One similar tale was about Mithras, a Persian warrior-god whose cults flourished just before the time of Jesus. Early Christians associated the two, and Roman soldiers referred to Mithras as "the Soldier's Christ."[2] In addition, Jesus was supposed to have raised Lazarus from the dead, so it would have been natural to ask, "If Jesus could raise Lazarus, why couldn't God raise Jesus?" Finally, even if the story of resurrection was new, "new" does not imply "true." So it is hardly clear that the tomb was empty.

Suppose it was empty. There are still (at least!) two possibilities: (1) Jesus' body disappeared and rose into heaven, or (2) someone took the body without being caught. Which is more likely? The answer is obvious, because lots of items are taken without the thief being caught. In this case, the women were supposed to have found the door open and a person inside. (Mark 16:4–5) If so, many people had motive and opportunity to move the body. On the other hand, we have tons of evidence that bodies do not disappear and rise into heaven. Craig claims that Jesus' resurrection is *"plausible," "in accord with accepted beliefs,"* and *"not ad hoc."* (25) To the con-

trary, nothing could be more *ad hoc* than a unique exception to otherwise accepted physical principles. Just imagine that I return from
a hard day at the office to find that my favorite ice cream, which I
had saved for tonight, is gone from my refrigerator. My wife and
kids all deny that they took it. They are honest. Still, I wouldn't seriously consider the possibility that my ice cream ascended into
heaven and sits at the right hand of Ben and Jerry. Analogously, nobody would think that about Jesus' body if they did not already believe in God. Any reasonable person who looks at the evidence without prejudice would conclude that either the tomb was not empty
or someone took the body, even if we don't know which.

Similar considerations apply to Craig's claim, "On multiple occa-
sions and under various circumstances, different individuals and
groups of people experienced appearances of Jesus alive from the
dead." (23) Craig describes these reports as "independent," (23) but
how can he possibly know that some of his supposed witnesses did
not hear stories about the others? There were years for these stories to spread. Once one person claimed to see Jesus, it would naturally have become a badge of honor for anyone to make similar
claims. In these circumstances, the multiplication of proclamations
hardly "guarantees" (23) anything. I cannot explain every one of these
reports, because there is so little evidence and so much uncertainty
about the circumstances. Nonetheless, these gaps in our knowledge
are no reason to give up well-established physics on the basis of
decades-old reports by self-interested parties who faced social pressures and promptings with predispositions to believe. Craig's burden of proof cannot be carried by such feeble testimony.

3. Experiences

Religious beliefs are sometimes based not on testimony by others
but on religious experiences *of the believer*. The question then is
whether personal religious experiences provide adequate reasons to
believe in God.

There is no doubt that many people have experiences that seem
to them to come from a higher power outside of themselves. The
problem is that *too many* people have such experiences. Different
people with different religious beliefs have different experiences that
seem to come from different gods, even though the experiences seem

quite similar from the inside. The resulting beliefs conflict, so they cannot all be right. Indeed, the majority of them must be wrong, if only Christian experiences are correct, as traditional Christians claim. It follows that religious experience in general cannot be reliable, according to the Christian perspective itself.

Religious experiences also occur only when emotions run high and only to those who were predisposed to believe. Analogously, many people think that they see and hear ghosts when they are filled with fear and already believed in ghosts. These experiences are no evidence for the existence of ghosts, because they depend on emotions and prior belief. The same sources of error permeate religious experience. Craig says, "If you're sincerely seeking God, God will make his existence evident to you." (28) No surprise there! Take a pinch of belief in God, add a dash of desire to experience God, stir in emotion to taste, and you have a recipe for religious experience. This recipe has been franchised by preachers who induce religious experiences during worship services and elaborated by ascetics who starve themselves in order to see God. The problem is that such recipes work regardless of whether or not there is any God to cause the experience. That is why such experiences are *not* reliable indicators of God.

Some religious experiences might occur in circumstances that are more conducive to reliability. Indeed, some particular religious experiences might be accurate. I do not deny that this is *possible*. The point here is about *evidence*. Disagreement, prejudice, and emotion are so widespread in religion that any religious experience needs independent confirmation. To understand why, imagine three friends camping in the woods late one night. Ann believes that bears live nearby, so she bets that the next animal they see will be a bear. Betty thinks that the area is filled with deer, so she bets on a deer. Cathy refuses to be a part of their stupid bet. Then Ann looks deep into the forest. She sees a dark object. It moves. She thinks it is a bear. Betty sees the same dark object, but she thinks it is a deer. Cathy looks carefully at the same spot, but she sees only shadows. Given their disagreements, predispositions, and motivations, Ann is not justified in believing that she really saw a bear any more than Betty is justified in believing that she really saw a deer. If they find bear tracks in the morning, then they will have independent confirmation. Without independent confirmation, however, either one might be right, but neither one has enough evidence for justified belief or knowledge. Why? Because known disagreement, along with reliance on emotion and predisposition, creates the need for independent confirmation. The same standards should apply to religious experience and belief, so religious believers also need independent confirmation that their experiences are accurate or reliable.

Craig denies this when he claims that religious beliefs based on religious experience are "properly basic." (26) As examples of properly basic beliefs, Craig refers to "the belief in the reality of the past, the existence of the external world, and the presence of other minds like your own." (26) Such beliefs "aren't based on" any other beliefs and "are part of the foundation of a person's system of beliefs." (26) That makes them *basic*, but it does not explain what makes it *proper* to treat these beliefs as basic, that is, to believe them without any confirmation. So what does make them *properly* basic? Craig's first answer is that "none of these beliefs can be proved." (26) However, he cannot say this about religious beliefs, since he is trying to give arguments for God. Besides, even if they *cannot* be proved, that is not enough to show that they *need not* be confirmed. I also cannot prove that there is life on Mars, but that does not make me justified in accepting this belief without any evidence. Craig's second answer is better: "You would have to be crazy to" reject beliefs that there was a past, there is an external world, and there are other minds; and that makes these beliefs "*properly* basic." (26–27) But then a belief in God cannot be properly basic in the same way, unless "you would have to be crazy to" be an atheist. Even if you disagree with me, I hope you don't think I'm crazy. At least, not all atheists are crazy. So Craig has no good reason to claim that religious beliefs are properly basic.

In the absence of any better argument, there is no reason to deny and much reason to agree that religious beliefs need independent confirmation. Can this need be satisfied in the religious case? I don't see how. God leaves no tracks or other physical evidence, as a bear does. We cannot appeal to the internal character of religious experience, because the same kind of experience can be produced without God. Thus, the need for independent confirmation in religion cannot be met. But the need persists. That is why people are not justified in basing their religious beliefs on their religious experiences.

4. Origins

The remaining two arguments, which Craig gave first, are more abstract and technical. That is why I saved them for last. One is cosmological. The other is teleological.

Craig's cosmological argument is that "God makes sense of the origin of the universe." (3) The basic premises are: (1) the universe had a beginning, (2) God explains that beginning, and (3) nothing else explains that beginning as well. I doubt all three premises, but all I need to show here is that one or more of these premises is not supported by enough reason for us to be justified in believing that it is true. If even one premise is unjustified, the whole argument fails to justify belief in God.

Let's start with premise (1). To support (1), Craig uses mathematical and scientific twists and turns.

4.1. Mathematical Twists

Craig argues that the universe must have had a beginning, because it cannot be infinite. Why not? Craig answers, "[W]hat is infinity minus infinity? Well, mathematically, you get self-contradictory answers. . . . [I]nfinity minus infinity is infinity . . . [and] infinity minus infinity is 3! . . . This implies that infinity is just an idea in your mind, not something that exists in reality." (4)

This argument never mentions minds or reality before its conclusion. Its premises refer only to numbers. Consequently, if the argument showed anything about infinity, it would also show that there cannot be an infinite number or an infinite series of numbers. If the number itself or our idea of it implied a contradiction, there could not be any such number or any consistent idea of it. Calculus would be out the window. Let's hope that we can avoid that result.

Luckily, we can. Craig derives his contradiction by subtracting infinity from infinity. How do mathematicians avoid this contradiction? They simply limit the operation of subtraction to a certain domain, so that you are not allowed to subtract infinity. Why not? Because it gets you into contradictions! What better reason could you want? There is nothing strange or dubious about this limit on subtraction. Mathematicians also limit the operation of division. You can't divide any number by zero. Why not? Because this would also yield contradictions. That does not show that zero is not a number or is not real. The actual number of pink elephants in this room really is zero, believe me. So the limit on subtraction also does not show that infinity is not a number or is not real or is only in your mind or anything like that.

I admit that infinity is puzzling. It seems strange that the number of odd integers is equal to the total number of integers (both odd and even) in the sense that there is a one-to-one correspondence between the members of the sets. That's weird. But it is not contradictory. So this can't show that infinity does not exist in reality (whatever that means).

Many people's views on infinity do lead to outright contradictions. Even some mathematicians bungle it and end up claiming that actual infinities are impossible. Craig quotes David Hilbert, who was a great mathematician, but Craig's appeal takes an authority out of context. Craig's quotation is from a paper published in 1926.[3] Hilbert himself soon recognized that his finitist project was undermined by Gödel's incompleteness theorems in 1931.[4] More importantly, even if Hilbert had not recanted (or reCantored?), almost all mathematicians today recognize that infinity can be handled without contradiction. If you want to see how, just take a mathematics course on real analysis.

Craig might admit that infinity is not self-contradictory, but still deny that anything infinite actually exists. However, actual infinities are not hard to find. First, there is an infinite number of real numbers between one and two. Craig cites one mathematician who regards this set as "merely *potentially* infinite," because "such series approach infinity as a limit, but they never actually get there." (7) This spatial metaphor is misleading. If I count to 10 and then stop, I potentially count to 20, but I do not actually count to 20. That fact does not even begin to show that the number 20 is not real. The number 20 actually exists whether or not my counting actually gets there. Some numbers are so high that nobody has ever counted to them or could ever count to them. Maybe we can "never actually get there," but the number series itself actually exists anyway.[5] The same goes for infinity. If someone asked how many real numbers exist between one and two, the answer would be, "Actually, it's infinite."

Craig later adds, "existence in the mathematical realm does not imply existence in the real world." (7) Is he denying the reality of numbers? On what basis? Anyway, even if numbers did not count (ha!), actual infinities also abound in the physical world. To see one, just wave your hand. When your hand moves a foot (ha, again!), it goes through an infinite number of intervening segments: half, then half of that, then half of that, and so on. It also travels for half the time, half of that, and so on. Craig again claims that this "confuses a potential infinite with an actual infinite," (7) but he is the one who is confused. We cannot measure or distinguish all of these spatial and temporal segments, but that does not show that they do not actually exist. These areas of space and periods of time really exist, regardless of our limitations and actions. When you think them through, such simple experiments are enough to reveal actual infinities "in the real world." Consequently, no mathematical argument could show that the universe cannot also be infinite.[6]

4.2. Scientific Turns

Craig also cites Big Bang theories as empirical evidence for a first moment and, hence, against an infinite past and, eventually, for God. Claims like this have been common since a Big Bang theory was first developed by a priest named Lemaitre. In 1951, Pope Pius XII cited this Big Bang theory as evidence for God. Lemaitre responded, "As far as I can see, such a theory remains entirely outside any metaphysical or religious question. It leaves the materialist free to deny any transcendental Being. . . . For the believer, it removes any attempt to familiarity with God."[7] Craig is no more justified than the Pope in inferring God from the Big Bang.

One reason is that Craig's inference to God depends on a questionable interpretation of the physics of the Big Bang. Craig emphasizes, "Physical space and time were created in that event, as well as all the matter and energy in the universe," (4) so there was no time or space or matter or energy at all in any form before the Big Bang. Some scientists do talk this way, but none of this speculation is essential to the physics or required by the evidence. That is why contrary hypotheses, such as a non-empty quantum epoch (discussed below), are still seen as live options that are not ruled out by the evidence.[8] But then why do any scientists deny time before the Big Bang? They are talking about time *as we know it*. When Hawking is more careful, he says, "the *classical* concepts of space and time break down as do all *known* laws of physics."[9] We cannot know any-thing about time before the Big Bang, and no claim about time before the Big Bang is needed or could be used to explain or predict anything that we observe now. Still, none of this implies that there was no time at all in any form before the Big Bang (*when* was that?). Scientists *ig-nore* temporal relations that are needless, useless, and unknowable, but to go further and *deny* such relations is at best conjecture. It is not re-quired by theory or evidence. We just can't know one way or the other.

When physicists do speculate on such matters, they adopt differ-ing views. Some say that before the Big Bang all space, time, mat-ter, and energy were collapsed into a point called a singularity. This singularity is a unique sort of reality, but it is still real,[10] if only be-cause it has infinite density. So even this theory does not require creation out of nothing. (Slogan: Singularity forever!)

Most physicists today reject the idea of a singularity. One reason is that recent discoveries produce doubts that gravity is always at-tractive, which is a key assumption in the argument for a singular-ity. Instead of a singularity, many physicists propose that the classi-cal epoch governed by classical physical laws began with the Big Bang, but before that was a quantum epoch with no beginning. All that existed during this quantum epoch was "a sea of fluctuating en-ergy," but it was "not nothing." (6) The Big Bang then arose prob-abilistically with no determinate cause, in some way analogous to the decay of radioactive atoms according to quantum theory. Hence the name "quantum epoch."

In response, Craig denies that any event can be uncaused, but this claim is contrary to standard quantum theory. Craig is right that "not all scientists agree that [some] sub-atomic events are uncaused," (6) but many scientists do agree with this. The lack of universal agree-ment hardly shows that most scientists are wrong to postulate un-caused events, and the fact that some scientists accept Craig's prem-ise is hardly enough for a positive argument for God. On the other issue here, Craig is also right that indeterministic quantum theory does not imply that particles come into existence out of nothing. (6) However, the quantum epoch's "sea of fluctuating energy" is also not nothing, even if we cannot know what it is. Thus, the principle that nothing comes from nothing creates no trouble for the hy-pothesis of a quantum epoch.

Anyway, I do not need to claim that there was a quantum epoch. My point is only that we cannot rule out a quantum epoch. It is as likely as other hypotheses. We just don't know which hypothesis is true. Our ignorance is confirmed by many recent fundamental developments and discoveries in this area. As recently as February 8, 2001, while I was finishing this chapter, scientists announced their discovery of previously unknown particles lurking in the sub-atomic sea that is supposed to resemble the quantum epoch. These results seem to undermine the Standard Model of sub-atomic physics and might affect theories about the origin of the universe. But nobody knows yet. Only one thing is clear: When so little is known, this is a very shaky foundation for any argument, despite all of Craig's footnotes.

Many mysteries remain. Maybe no physical theory will ever fully solve them all. But God won't solve them either. Here's why: A cause of an event is supposed to explain why that event occurred when it did rather than earlier or later and in the way it did rather than some other way. God cannot explain why the Big Bang occurred 15 billion years ago instead of 5 or 25 billion years ago, because, if the traditional God exists at all, He existed equally and in exactly the same way 5, 15, and 25 billion years ago. Furthermore, the hypothesis of God cannot explain why the Big Bang has any of the features it has, since, if the Big Bang had different features, God would be just as good (or bad) at explaining those other features. I will develop these points in Chapter 4, but it should already be clear why an eternal God adds nothing to the scientific explanations. To cite God as the cause of the Big Bang is to explain the obscure by the more obscure, which gets us nowhere.

Craig sketches the beginnings of a response when he argues that the cause of the Big Bang "must also be personal. For how else could a timeless cause give rise to a temporal effect like the universe?" (5) I agree that there is no *other* way, since there is *no* way, even for persons. Persons live within time. Yesterday at 6:00 p.m. I chose to order a pizza. As soon as it arrived (no earlier and no later), I willed to take my first bite. All such decisions must occur at some time rather than another. Otherwise, I could never order pizza again at a different time (which would be sad). Thus, it makes no sense when Craig says, "A man sitting from eternity could freely will to stand up." (6) A decision to stand up occurs at a specific time, but an eternal being exists outside time, so a truly eternal or "timeless" being cannot choose to sit up or do anything else. Even if there could be decisions outside of time, they could not explain why an event occurs when it does instead of at some earlier or later time, since a timeless decision would not occur at (or before) one time instead of another. So eternal beings cannot be causes, even if they are persons.

Craig tries to avoid these problems by saying, "God existing alone without the universe is either (i) before the Big Bang, not in physical time, but in an undifferentiated metaphysical time or else (ii) strictly timeless but that He enters into time at the moment of creation. I am not aware of any incoherence in either of these alternatives." (8) They both seem incoherent to me. If something is "strictly timeless" by its very nature, how can it ever "enter into time"? And if "undifferentiated metaphysical time" is time, then there was *some* kind of time before the Big Bang. Metaphysical time is "not nothing." So I don't see how either of these moves can help the traditional God make sense of the origin of the universe.

A lot is unknown here, so one final point is perhaps worth adding. Craig says, "both of the premises of the first argument thus seem more plausible than their denials. Hence, it is plausible that a transcendent Creator of the universe exists." (8) This does not follow. Compare this argument: When I pick a card from a standard deck without looking, (1) it is not a spade, (2) it is not a heart, (3) it is not a diamond, (4) it is not a club, so (5) it is not any suit. The conclusion, (5), is obviously false, even though each premise taken individually has a probability of 3/4, so each premise is more plausible than its denial, which has a probability of 1/4. Analogously, Craig's conclusion might be implausible, even if each of his premises taken individually is more plausible than its denial. Small doubts about each premise can accumulate into large doubts about the conclusion. Anyway, no such subtlety is needed here, where large doubts about each premise accumulate into even larger doubts about Craig's conclusion.[11]

5. Tuning Out

Craig's next argument also concerns the beginning of our universe, but from a different angle. The issue now is fine-tuning.

Intelligent life depends on "a complex and delicate balance of initial conditions." (9) Craig claims that God explains this fine-tuning, because God is supposed to have designed these conditions to serve His purpose. Without a designer, the occurrence of just the right conditions for intelligent life looks like an unlikely cosmic coincidence. This is supposed to show that God is the best explanation of the fine-tuning and of intelligent life, so God exists.

To support the crucial premise that intelligent life is improbable without a designer, Craig appeals to very big numbers "until our minds are reeling." (10) These probabilities are suspect. We can calculate the probability of picking an ace out of a deck if we know that the deck includes 4 aces in 52 cards. We cannot determine the probability of picking an ace out of a random pile of cards if we have no idea how many cards or aces are in the pile. Analogously, there is no non-arbitrary way to count either the total number of possible values for initial conditions in the universe (infinite?) or the range of values that could support some form of life (given interactions among factors). Thus, there is no way to calculate reliable probabilities here.[12]

Nonetheless, let's grant that intelligent life is improbable. This assumption alone would hardly imply a designer. In a big lottery, if you buy only one ticket, it is unlikely that you will win. Still, if you do win, you wouldn't conclude that God (or anyone else) must have fixed the lottery in your favor. You might just have been lucky. Similarly, when you win the lottery of life, there is no reason to infer that God or any designer exists. The same response applies regardless of how many tickets were sold, and regardless of whether your numbers fit some pattern, so Craig's big numbers (9) and talk about patterns (11) cannot save his argument.

Craig responds by substituting a different lottery that might have no winner "in which a single white ball is mixed into a billion billion billion black balls, and you are asked to reach in and pull out a ball." (12) Suppose you pick the white ball. You would and should be very surprised; but you still should not jump to the conclusion that the lottery was rigged, if you have no reason to assume that anyone was in a position to rig the lottery. A house in Connecticut is reported to have been hit by two meteors years apart. If the reports are true, this coincidence is very unlikely, but it hardly shows that God is throwing stones at that house.

It might be reasonable to conclude that the lottery was fixed if you had independent reason to believe that someone had opportunity and motive to fix it. If you already know a lottery official who likes you, then it might make sense to suppose that this official made you win. However, the analogous assumption in the fine-tuning argument would be that God had an opportunity and motive to rig the universe in our favor. That assumption would blatantly beg the question in an argument for the existence of God. Thus, although the fine-tuning argument might seem convincing to theists who already assume that God was there to design the universe, the argument itself gives them no reason to believe that assumption.

Craig might complain that atheists also beg the question if they assume that there was no God to fix the lottery of life. Atheists do not need this assumption, however, because they are not arguing against God (yet). They are (so far) merely criticizing Craig's argument. To refute an argument, one need not show that its premises are false. It is enough to show that its premises are unjustified. Thus, all that atheists need to claim (so far) is that fine-tuning leaves open the question of whether or not there is a designer.

This point can be made more technically by distinguishing likelihood from conditional probability. The likelihood of fine-tuning and intelligent life, given that a traditional God exists, seems high. Nonetheless, the probability of such a God, given that intelligent life exists, still might be low. To see which figure is relevant, consider another analogy: The likelihood of hearing noises in your attic, given that there are ghosts in your attic, is high. In contrast, the probability of ghosts, given noises in your attic, is low. This low probability shows why noises give you no good reason to believe in ghosts, even if you have no other explanation for the noises. The point is not that ghosts are inherently improbable, but only that there are too many other possibilities to justify jumping to the conclusion that ghosts caused the noise, without assuming that there are ghosts in the area. You also should not believe that the noises were caused by bats until you have additional independent reason to assume that there are bats in the area (and that the noise was caused by bats as opposed to squirrels, birds, wind, and so on). Analogously, intelligent life is no evidence for God, even if we have no other explanation for intelligent life, unless we assume that God was there to design the universe. But that assumption would beg the question.

Some atheists disagree. They admit that belief in God *would* be justified *if* we had no other explanation for fine-tuning. Craig's argument still fails, however, because several competing explanations are available: (1) the Christian God, (2) one Big Bang and only chance, and (3) multiple cosmoi, each with its own Big Bang. If there are enough cosmoi, it becomes probable that at least one contains intelligent life. We live in one that does. That should come as no surprise, since otherwise we would not be alive to tell the tale.

Craig rejects this multiple-cosmoi hypothesis as "arguably inferior to the design hypothesis, because the design hypothesis is *simpler*." (13) However, the multiple-cosmoi hypothesis postulates more tokens of the same type (Big Bangs), whereas the design hypothesis postulates a wholly new type of thing (God). What matters is new types, not new tokens. To see this, compare a scientist who postulates a wholly new type of element when the evidence can be explained just as well by postulating only new samples of the same old types of elements. This scientist's new-element hypothesis would and should be rejected as less simple than the old-elements hypothesis. For the same reasons, the God hypothesis should be rejected as less simple than the multiple-cosmoi hypothesis.

In addition, fine-tuning might be explained by another recent hypothesis: (4) tracker fields.[13] In tracker fields, so-called constants adjust toward the values that make matter and life possible. As a result, matter and life would occur no matter which of a wide range of values these constants had at the time of the Big Bang. This makes intelligence more intelligible.

These scientific hypotheses are not merely on the same footing as the hypothesis of God. Evidence supports them because they follow from theories that make predictions that have been confirmed.[14] No such observational evidence supports the hypothesis of God.

I am not endorsing either (3) multiple cosmoi or (4) tracker fields. Both hypotheses face problems. Craig is right that we do not know how multiple cosmoi or tracker fields are generated. (13–14) There are also many mysteries about the rate of evolution, which Craig mentions, (15) although punctuated equilibrium theory helps here.

However, none of these persistent puzzles proves God. That would be a bad argument from ignorance. We just don't know enough in this area to supply stable support for belief in God.

It is hard for us to admit our own ignorance. We evolved with a strong urge to seek explanations for what otherwise seems random. Nonetheless, we should not jump to supernatural explanations as a quick fix for ignorance. Such appeals to God cause more trouble in the long term, because they cut short inquiry. If God fine-tuned the initial conditions, it would be pointless to seek any deeper explanation, such as tracker fields. In contrast, when atheists ascribe fine-tuning to chance, they admit the possibility of deeper explanations. This stimulates inquiry that increases our knowledge while also raising new questions that themselves demand further answers. This useful process is undercut when observations are explained by postulating God. In this way, religious beliefs get in the way of science and the progress of knowledge.

These objections undermine Craig's argument, even if the design hypothesis would explain fine-tuning. But it wouldn't. No matter what happens, one can always postulate someone who designed things that way. If the universe expands, God designed it to expand. If the universe contracts, God designed it to contract. Since God could design it either way, the hypothesis of God cannot explain why anything happens one way rather than another. Moreover, the design hypothesis works only if God can cause changes to tune the universe for life. I argued in section 4.2 that an eternal God cannot cause such changes in our temporal world, and I will develop that point in Chapter 4. The design hypothesis, thus, becomes incoherent if the designer is supposed to be an eternal God.

6. Conclusions

Craig has not given us any adequate reason to believe either in a divine source of morality or in the resurrection of Jesus or in a superhuman cause of religious experience or in a creator or designer of the universe. Moreover, Craig's conclusions are bloated. Even if Craig's arguments did establish some conclusions, they would not show the existence of God with all of His traditional features. In particular, even if some commander did dictate morality, that commander still might not be good or have the power to punish disobedience by humans. Even if Jesus did rise from the dead, maybe he was abducted by aliens or maybe raising Jesus tired out God, so God lost His power. Even if religious experiences were some evidence for some external source, the most vivid religious experience could result from a God who is only very strong and pretty good. Even if some creator or designer could be proven, this creator or designer might have died a long time ago. Indeed, if God designed this universe, there is much reason to doubt that He is all-good, as we will see in Chapter 4. For such reasons, nothing like the traditional God would follow even if Craig's arguments did work part way.

Craig might respond that all of his arguments work together. However, the combined set still would not show all of the traditional features of God, since none establishes that God is all-powerful. If there were a creator, that creator would have to be *very* powerful, but need not be able to control *all* small-scale events for *all* time. Moreover, even if all of God's features were covered, it would still not be clear that Craig's different arguments are about the same being, since a creator might be separate from the commander of morality and also from the source of religious experience. To assume identity is just another way to bloat conclusions.

There always might be better arguments for the existence of God. Theologians are inventive. However, until someone gives a better argument, we have no good reason to believe that a traditional God exists.

Notes

1. I refer to God as "He" because Craig and other traditional theologians use this masculine pronoun, although, as many have pointed out, it is not clear how God could have any gender.

2. Thanks to Susan Ackerman for this information.

3. David Hilbert, "Über das Unendliche," *Mathematische Annalen* 95 (Berlin, 1926): 161–90. Craig cites a reprint of a translation.

4. Kurt Gödel, "Über formal unendscheidbare Sätze der *Principia Mathematica* und verwandter Systeme I," *Monatshefte für Mathematik und Physik* 38 (1931). Thanks to Sam Levey for help on this paragraph and elsewhere.

5. Mathematical constructivists might deny this, but Craig is no constructivist, and it is hard to imagine any good reason to be a constructivist about numbers if you believe in God, since constructivism is motivated by skepticism about entities like gods.

6. For more detailed criticisms of Craig's mathematical arguments, see

Quentin Smith, "Infinity and the Past" in William Lane Craig and Quentin Smith, *Theism, Atheism, and Big Bang Cosmology* (Oxford: Clarendon Press, 1993).

7. Quoted in Marcelo Gleiser, *The Dancing Universe: From Creation Myths to the Big Bang* (New York: Penguin, 1997), 287. Thanks to Marcelo Gleiser for help at several points in sections 4.2 and 5.

8. Craig does criticize this theory: "Vacuum Fluctuation Universe theories . . . cannot explain why, if the vacuum was eternal, we do not observe an infinitely old universe." (8) However, the universe that we observe is (in a way) infinitely old in this view, even if its classical phase (which is the phase that we observe) is not infinitely old. So it is not clear what Craig's objection is.

9. S. W. Hawking, "Breakdown of Predictability in Gravitational Collapse," *Physical Review* D14 (1976): 2460 (my emphasis).

10. On the reality of a singularity, see Quentin Smith in Craig and Smith, *Theism, Atheism, and Big Bang Cosmology*, p. 208.

11. For more detailed criticisms of Craig's scientific arguments, see Quentin Smith, "Atheism, Theism, and Big Bang Cosmology" and "A Defense of the Cosmological Argument for God's Non-existence" in Craig and Smith, *Theism, Atheism, and Big Bang Cosmology* (chaps. VII and IX).

12. On the technical problems with calculating these probabilities, see Timothy McGrew, Lydia McGrew, and Eric Vestrup, "Probabilities and the Fine-Tuning Argument: A Sceptical View," *Mind* 110 (2001): 1027–1037.

13. Jeremiah Ostriker and Paul J. Steinhardt, "The Quintessential Universe," *Scientific American* 284 (2001): 51–52. Tracker fields are just one example of a dynamical system in which physical observables, responding in part to feedback with the environment, evolve inevitably toward a certain final state, which is insensitive to the initial conditions. Tracker fields make fine-tuning understandable in the same way as do many other such dynamical systems throughout nature. Thanks are due to Rob Caldwell here and at other points in this chapter.

14. Ibid.; on multiple cosmoi, see Alan Guth, *The Inflationary Universe* (Reading, Mass.: Addison-Wesley, 1997), 245–252.

CHAPTER 3

Reason Enough

William Lane Craig

Introductory Remarks

In my opening essay, I presented five reasons why I think that theism is more plausibly true than atheism. I'm grateful for Walter Sinnott-Armstrong's stimulating and engaging interaction with those arguments. Far from being a "shotgun" approach, as he alleges, my five reasons to believe that God exists constitute a progressive, systematic case for Christian theism. With each argument, we learn more about the ultimate ground of our existence: that there is a Personal Creator and Intelligent Designer of the universe, Who is the locus of moral value, Who has revealed Himself in Jesus Christ, and Who can be known in personal experience. Mine is a cumulative case for the existence of God, both in the sense that the arguments reinforce one another and in the sense that they supplement one another in order to arrive at the traditional concept of God. In assessing Sinnott-Armstrong's criticisms, I'm therefore going to stick by the order in which I initially presented the arguments rather than follow his re-ordering.

But before I look at his criticisms in detail, I want to say a word about each of the three fallacies I allegedly commit, which Sinnott-Armstrong playfully labels the fallacies of "bloated conclusions," "false dichotomy," and "excessive footnotes."

First, do I commit the fallacy of bloated conclusions? When Sinnott-Armstrong alleges this, he isn't referring to the specific conclusions of my individual five arguments themselves. Those conclusions do follow from the premises. Rather he is claiming that even if all my arguments are sound, they do not suffice to justify the conclusion that God exists. Perhaps a Creator or a Designer of the universe exists, but such a being does not deserve to be called "God." I guess that depends on what you mean by "God." Sinnott-Armstrong seems to forget that my case is a cumulative one: taken together, the arguments, if successful, do enable us to recover a striking number of the traditional divine attributes. The first argument gives us a Personal Creator of the universe who is uncaused, eternal, changeless (at least *sans* the universe), immaterial, and enormously powerful; the second gives us His inestimable intelligence and personal concern for intelligent creatures; the third, His absolute goodness and love as well as His metaphysical necessity; the fourth, His identity with the God of Israel revealed by Jesus of Nazareth; and the fifth, His knowability. Together the arguments do, if successful, give us a full-orbed conception of God. They give us the God of the Bible.[1] It would be a strange form of atheism, indeed, which conceded that the God of the Bible exists! Clearly, if there is such a being, then atheism, in any reasonable sense of the term, is false.

Second, what about the fallacy of drawing false dichotomies? Again, no such fallacy is committed in my first three arguments, since they are logically valid, deductive arguments, whose conclusions follow necessarily from their premises. Since these arguments are logically valid, the only question is whether their premises are more plausibly true than their negations. Of the three, only the argument for design employs disjunctive reasoning, and its first premise states, not a dichotomy, but a trichotomy, a trichotomy that Sinnott-Armstrong does not challenge, as we'll see below. He has simply misstated my cosmological and moral arguments. As for my fourth, inductive argument concerning the historical Jesus, the form of this argument is inference to the best explanation. My contention is that given the historical facts of Jesus' honorable burial, the discovery of his empty tomb, the post-mortem appearances of Jesus, and the origin of the disciples' belief in his resurrection, the best explanation of these facts, when judged by such criteria as explanatory power, explanatory scope, plausibility, accord with accepted beliefs, absence of ad hoc hypotheses, and so on, is the hypothesis "God raised

Jesus from the dead." I by no means exclude other explanations from the pool of live options; I merely maintain that the Resurrection Hypothesis is the best. And, of course, one may dispute the historical facts themselves, and I'm prepared to discuss the various lines of evidence supporting each one. Thus, the charge that I commit the fallacy of drawing false dichotomies is very odd and must arise from inattentiveness to my formulation of the various arguments.

Finally, the charge of excessive footnotes! This is really the charge of a fallacious appeal to authority. But as Wesley Salmon puts it, "there are correct uses of authority and well as incorrect ones. It would be a sophomoric mistake to suppose that every appeal to authority is illegitimate, for the proper use of authority plays an indispensable role in the accumulation and application of knowledge."[2] In order to count as evidence, the testimony must be from an honest and reliable authority on a matter in the person's field of expertise. In that case, "The appeal to a reliable authority is legitimate, for the testimony of a reliable authority is evidence for the conclusion."[3] Thus, while a Hollywood starlet's endorsement of a commercial product does not count as evidence, the expert testimony of a DNA specialist concerning blood found at the scene of a crime does. When I quote recognized authorities like Hawking, Ruse, Kremer, Johnson, and others concerning matters in their respective fields of expertise, particularly about the state of scholarly opinion in their fields, this most certainly does count as expert testimony and, hence, evidence for the matter in question. I might note in this connection that Sinnott-Armstrong's dismissal of scholarly opinion concerning the empty tomb of Jesus on the grounds of "bias" is quite naïve. As the New Testament scholar R. T. France points out with respect to the historical study of the four Gospels, "Ancient historians have sometimes observed that the degree of skepticism with which New Testament scholars approach their sources is far greater than would be thought justified in any other branch of ancient history. Indeed, many ancient historians would count themselves fortunate to have four such responsible accounts, written within a generation or two of the events, and preserved in such a wealth of manuscript evidence."[4] Ironically, Sinnott-Armstrong himself not infrequently recurs to expert testimony in his criticisms, though I am struck by the weakness of that testimonial evidence (e.g., the information on Mithraism communicated to him by one Susan Ackerman). Of course, the ultimate question concerns the evidence upon which scholarly opinion is based, and I'm more than ready to discuss that evidence.

With these preliminaries out of the way, let's now get down to a detailed examination of my arguments and Sinnott-Armstrong's criticisms of them. I propose that we look at the arguments one premise at a time.

Cosmological Argument

My first reason, that *God Makes Sense of the Origin of the Universe*, is a version of the cosmological argument. Sinnott-Armstrong discusses it in section 4 of his response. Attentive readers will notice how seriously misstated his rendition of my argument in his second paragraph is. Let's look at the argument as I actually formulated it.

1. Whatever Begins to Exist Has a Cause

Sinnott-Armstrong replies, "Craig denies that any event can be uncaused, but this is contrary to standard quantum theory." Both clauses of this sentence are, unfortunately, misrepresentations.

First, the clause "Craig denies that any event can be uncaused" misrepresents premise (1), which has nothing to do with events at all, but with things. It states that things do not come into existence without a cause. The premise is fully compatible with events happening without a cause and so leaves that question open. What it denies is that things pop into being without causes.

The second clause, "this is contrary to standard quantum theory," misrepresents quantum theory. Any physical theory is comprised of two parts: a mathematical formulation and a physical interpretation of the mathematical formulas. While the mathematical core of quantum theory has been confirmed to a fantastic degree of precision, there are at least ten different physical interpretations of the mathematics, and no one knows which of these, if any, is correct, since they are all empirically equivalent.[5] Only some of these, principally the so-called Copenhagen Interpretation, are causally indeterministic. Others are fully deterministic. In order to show that quantum theory proves that events can happen without causes, Sinnott-Armstrong would have to show that these other interpretations of quantum theory are not as good as the Copenhagen Interpretation, which is, of course, impossible to do.

Moreover, even in the Copenhagen Interpretation things don't come into being without a cause. It's true that in this interpretation so-called virtual particles can arise spontaneously out of the quantum vacuum. But Sinnott-Armstrong recognizes that the quantum vacuum is not nothing; rather it's a sea of fluctuating energy that serves as the indeterministic cause of such virtual particles. The philosopher of science Bernulf Kanitscheider emphasizes with respect to quantum vacuum models of the origin of the universe,

> The violent microstructure of the vacuum has been used in attempts to explain the origin of the universe as a long-lived vacuum fluctuation. . . . From the philosophical point of view it is essential to note that the foregoing is far from being a spontaneous generation of everything from naught, but the origin of that embryonic bubble is really a causal process leading from a primordial substratum with a rich physical structure to a materialized substratum of the vacuum. Admittedly this process is not deterministic, it includes that weak kind of causal dependence peculiar to every quantum mechanical process.[6]

Thus, even in the disputed Copenhagen Interpretation, the quantum vacuum is a physical cause of the entities it is alleged to spawn.

The bottom line is that if we think that things cannot just pop into being out of nothing, which surely seems reasonable, then quantum theory does not constitute a defeater of that premise.

2. The Universe Began to Exist

You'll recall that I presented both a philosophical argument as well as scientific evidence for this premise. Let's examine each in turn.

Philosophical Argument. Sinnott-Armstrong raises three objections to my philosophical argument for the finitude of the past:

1. *It would prove that there are not an infinite number of numbers.* Right! But this conclusion is problematic only if one is a Platonist, who believes that numbers are actually existing, mind-independent things. Mathematics doesn't commit us to Platonism, and existence claims in infinite set theory don't commit us to the mind-independent existence of such entities. As Kasner and Newman nicely put it, "the

infinite certainly does not exist in the same sense that we say, 'There are fish in the sea.' Existence in the mathematical sense is wholly different from the existence of objects in the physical world."[7] My claim here is that although infinite set theory and transfinite arithmetic each constitutes a logically consistent universe of discourse, given their axioms and conventions, the existence of an actual infinite in the real world leads to intolerable absurdities. My argument does not deny the coherence of that universe of discourse. Thus, we needn't fear that my argument will relieve undergraduates of learning the calculus!

2. *We can forbid mathematical operations on infinite quantities that lead to contradictions.* That works great in the postulated mathematical realm of discourse; but in the real world you can't stop people from taking away real objects or dividing real collections! Of course, "mathematicians today recognize that infinity can be handled without contradiction." They do so by axiomatization and conventional rules that are laid down for their abstract universe of discourse but which make no claim for the real world.[8] Sinnott-Armstrong's assertion that zero corresponds to a really existing entity seems confused: when we say that there are zero elephants in this room, we do not mean that there are elephants in this room, and the number of them is zero! Rather we mean that there just is no such entity in the room.

3. *There are counter-examples of really existing actual infinites.* Sinnott-Armstrong mentions two: (i) *The real numbers between 1 and 2.* To claim this as a bonafide counter-example presupposes that there are such mind-independent entities as numbers, which begs the question in favor of Platonism. And Sinnott-Armstrong says nothing to show that the intuitionists (or constructivists mentioned in his note 5), who deny even the mathematical existence of the actual infinite, are wrong. (ii) *The spacetime continuum.* The alleged counter-example of moving my hand across a distance presupposes that physical intervals are composed of an actually infinite number of points, which begs the question. If the interval is not a construction of points, but is logically prior to any divisions we care to make of it, then the potential infinite divisibility of the interval does not imply that it is divided into an actually infinite number of parts.

In presenting these putative counter-examples, I think that Sinnott-Armstrong has failed to understand the nature of what philosophers call "defeaters." Defeaters can be of two sorts: *rebutting defeaters*, which try to show that some position or statement is false, and *undercutting defeaters*, which try to show that a position or statement has not been shown to be true. The appeal to counter-examples is an attempt to offer a rebutting defeater. The counter-example is alleged to falsify the claim against which it is directed. In order to turn back the force of his alleged counter-examples, all I have to do is offer an undercutting defeater of his examples by showing that there are other equally good ways of construing them that do not involve commitment to actual infinites. I don't have to show his construal to be false but merely that he hasn't shown it alone to be true. It will then be up to Sinnott-Armstrong to show us why my construal isn't just as viable. It is he who bears the burden of proof to show that his alleged counter-examples *commit* us to the existence of actual, rather than merely potential, infinites; otherwise they do not defeat my argument against the actual infinite based on the absurdities that its real existence would lead to.

Hence, I really don't find any of these objections to my philosophical argument to be persuasive.

Scientific Evidence. Sinnott-Armstrong presents two objections to my appeal to the evidence of astrophysical cosmology for the beginning of the universe:

1. *The inference to God depends on a questionable interpretation of the physics.* First, it's important to realize that I make no inference to God from physics; that misimpression arises only from Sinnott-Armstrong's misstatement of my argument. Rather the physical evidence is adduced in support of the premise *The universe began to exist.* This is a religiously neutral statement, which may be found in almost any textbook on astrophysical cosmology.

Second, the issue is not whether the conclusion that the universe began to exist is "essential to the physics or required by the evidence," but whether the evidence makes that conclusion more plausibly true than its negation.[9] Sinnott-Armstrong really does the reader a disservice by wrongly suggesting that recent discoveries, which are wholly consonant with the Big Bang model, somehow cast doubt upon it.[10]

Third, Sinnott-Armstrong confuses two questions: (i) Does the Standard Model predict a beginning to the spacetime universe? And (ii) Is the prediction of the Standard Model correct? There is simply no ambiguity about the answer to (i). As I explained in my opening statement, in the Standard Model there is just nothing prior to the initial cosmological singularity. The beginning predicted by the Standard Model involves an initial cosmological singularity, which constitutes an edge or boundary to physical space and time. Physicists John Barrow and Frank Tipler emphasize, "At this singularity, space and time came into existence; literally nothing existed before the singularity, so, if the Universe originated at such a singularity, we would truly have a creation *ex nihilo*."[11]

As for (ii), while certainty is of course impossible here, it is noteworthy that every attempt to avert the absolute beginning predicted by the Standard Model has failed.[12] Models that seek to avert the prediction of the Standard Model of an absolute beginning of the universe have time and again been shown either to be untenable or else to imply the very beginning of the universe that their proponents sought to avoid. For example, the problem with the obsolete quantum vacuum models appealed to by Sinnott-Armstrong is that they predicted that universes would form at every point in the quantum vacuum, so that given an infinite past, universes would come into being at every point in the vacuum and would eventually all collide and coalesce into one infinitely old universe, which contradicts observation. Sinnott-Armstrong's response to this shortcoming shows that he doesn't get it. He says in his note 8, "the universe that we observe is (in a way) infinitely old in this view, even if its classical phase (which is the phase that we observe) is not infinitely old. So it is not clear what Craig's objection is." The objection is that in such theories we wouldn't be observing a young classical phase. For the various baby universes formed within the womb of the wider Mother Universe would, given infinite time, have all run into one another as they grew older and so merged into one tired, old universe, which contradicts our observation of a relatively young universe. According to Britain's leading quantum cosmologist, Christopher Isham, this difficulty proved "fairly lethal" to vacuum fluctuation models, and so they were "given up twenty years ago and nothing much has been done with them since."[13] Sinnott-Armstrong is therefore just incorrect to call such theories "as likely as other hypotheses." As for the recent discovery alluded to by Sinnott-Armstrong that the cosmic expansion is accelerating rather than decelerating, this startling development *supports* the beginning of the universe by further undermining the old oscillating model, since an accelerating expansion cannot reverse under the force of gravitation into a Big Crunch, but will proceed endlessly.

2. *Theism cannot explain the origin of the universe.* Notice that this objection is irrelevant to the truth of the second premise, that the universe began to exist. It is actually a criticism of my subsequent argument for the personhood of the First Cause. But let's go ahead and deal with it here. From the two premises, it follows that the universe has a cause. But is that cause personal or impersonal? Sinnott-Armstrong agrees that an impersonal, timeless cause cannot give rise to a temporal effect like the universe. But, he insists, neither can a personal cause, because no coherent doctrine of God's relationship to time can be formulated. I claimed, "God existing alone without the universe is either (i) before the Big Bang, not in physical time, but in an undifferentiated metaphysical time or else (ii) strictly timeless but . . . He enters into time at the moment of creation." Sinnott-Armstrong objects to (i) because then there was after all "*some* kind of time before the Big Bang." That's right; but this implication is scientifically inconsequential, since such a time would be a metaphysical reality that physical cosmology does not study. Hence, its existence would contradict no scientific evidence or theory. As for (ii), he objects that a being that is " 'strictly timeless' by its very nature" can never enter into time. This response illicitly presupposes that God's temporal status is an *essential*, rather than *contingent*, property of God, which is not incumbent upon the traditional theist. If God is contingently temporal or atemporal (as I happen to think), then His entering into time is not incompatible with His nature. For more on this very important issue, see our discussion of "The Problem of Action" in chapters 4–6.

Since my cosmological argument is a deductive argument, Sinnott-Armstrong's final animadversions concerning inductive arguments are irrelevant.

Teleological Argument

My second reason, that *God Makes Sense of the Fine-Tuning of the Universe for Intelligent Life*, is a form of the teleological argument. Sinnott-Armstrong treats it in section 5 of his response. Let's examine each of its premises.

1. The Fine-Tuning of the Universe Is Due to Either Law, Chance, or Design

This first premise presupposes that the universe is in fact fine-tuned for intelligent, carbon-based life and states the three possible explanations of this fact. Sinnott-Armstrong is skeptical that the universe is fine-tuned in the way that I describe. He is suspicious of the probabilities involved because, he claims, we have no non-arbitrary way of counting the total number of values that a constant or quantity could assume, nor the range of values that are life-permitting. This denial of the fact of fine-tuning is remarkable. Otherwise sober cosmologists are not beating one another out the back door to adopt metaphysically speculative scenarios of a World Ensemble for no good reason! As for Sinnott-Armstrong's misgivings, the range of life-permitting values can in many cases be confidently established because if the values were allowed to vary beyond a certain restricted range, neither stars nor planets could exist (not to speak of biological organisms) and in some cases none but the lightest elements and in certain cases not even matter itself.[14] As for estimating the range of possible values that the various constants and quantities might assume, we may take as our limit those values that are universe-permitting.[15] For example, if gravity were to have a value 10^{100} times its present value, there wouldn't even be a universe, but a mere singularity. Thus, we needn't worry about the range of possible values extending to infinity. When you compare the range of possible values of the fundamental quantities permitted by the laws of nature with the range of life-permitting values, you find either that the range of life-permitting values is exceedingly small in comparison with the wider range of assumable values or else that the actual value of some constant or quantity falls improbably close to the edge of the life-permitting range. Well-established cases of this sort of fine-tuning include the strong force, the weak force, the electromagnetic force, the gravitational force, the proton-neutron mass ratio, and the cosmological constant.[16] Fine-tuning is a scientifically established fact of nature that must be squarely faced.

Premise (1) states that there are only three alternatives available for explaining this remarkable fine-tuning: physical law, chance, or design. In his discussion, Sinnott-Armstrong tacitly admits that these are the only three alternatives. For of the "several competing alternatives" that he says are available to explain fine-tuning—namely, God, one Big Bang and chance alone, multiple universes each with its own Big Bang, or tracker fields—the first of these represents design, the second chance, the third chance again, and the fourth law. So the question is: which is the best explanation?

2. It Is Not Due to Law or Chance

Sinnott-Armstrong tends to conflate these two alternatives, asserting, "when atheists ascribe fine-tuning to chance, they admit the possibility of deeper explanations." This is incorrect; ascription to law allows deeper explanations, but chance takes the values of the variables to be brute facts, just inexplicable givens. The only thing the atheist can do in order to supplement the chance hypothesis is to multiply his probabilistic resources by positing the existence of a World Ensemble in order to make the odds of the existence of a life-permitting universe more tractable. Let's consider, then, these alternatives in order.

Law. Sinnott-Armstrong asserts that so-called tracker fields might explain fine-tuning. He refers here to the article in *Scientific American* on the acceleration of the cosmic expansion. The hypothetical field that drives the acceleration is called "quintessence." It has been speculated that this quintessence field tracks the matter fields in the expanding universe in such a way as to diminish a very large initial value of the cosmological constant to nearly zero today. It's immediately obvious that this hypothesis is, at face value, an attempt to explain merely one of the many finely tuned constants requisite for life, namely, the cosmological constant, and thus hardly constitutes an explanation of the universe's fine-tuning. In any case, some astrophysicists have complained that such a hypothetical field seems unacceptably ad hoc, and others have noted the severe problems facing such a proposed field.[17] Finally, Collins points out that "even if such a field were discovered, it would have to have just the right ('fine-tuned' or 'well-designed') mathematical form to overcome the severe problems facing such proposals. This would reintroduce the issue of fine-tuning and design at a different level, though in a mitigated way."[18] This has been the pattern with attempts to explain fine-tuning by physical law: Like a stubborn bump in the carpet, fine-tuning is suppressed at one point only to pop up at another. Quoting Carr and Rees to the effect that "even if all apparently anthropic coincidences could be explained [in terms of some grand unified theory], it would still be remarkable that the relationships dictated by physical theory happened also to be those propitious for life," Collins concludes, "It is very unlikely, therefore, that these cases of fine-tuning and others like them will lose their significance with the further development of science."[19]

Chance.   Sinnott-Armstrong presents two considerations in defense of chance.

1. *Improbability alone does not prove design.* Of course; I made that point myself. As I presented the argument, it's the combination of improbability with an independently given pattern that discredits chance. Imagine that Bob, who was born on August 8, 1948, receives a car for his birthday with the license plate BOB 8848. Would he be rational to shrug this off as due to chance on the ground that that combination of letters and numbers is as probable as any other? It is the combination of pattern and improbability that tips us off to design rather than chance. Given the independent pattern of variables necessary for life and the enormous improbability of those values obtaining in the Big Bang, the chance hypothesis is ruled out in favor of design.

Incredibly, Sinnott-Armstrong thinks that the unimaginable improbability of your picking a white ball rather than a black ball in the lottery I envisioned (where one white ball is mixed with a billion, billion, billion black balls, and you are given one pick) should not lead you to doubt that your picking white was the result of sheer chance! I take his intransigence on this score as illustrative of the willful blindness to which determined atheism leads. For this is a classic case of a design inference: since it is overwhelmingly more probable that your pick be black rather than white, you should reasonably conclude that your pick was not by chance. We can make this inference even more perspicuous without affecting the probabilistic features of the situation by imagining that you had to pick the one white ball several times in a row or you would be shot. Would any reasonable person who survived not think that the whole thing was rigged? Of course you would!

I presented the teleological argument using Dembski's analysis of design inferences. But an approach using the probability calculus is feasible as well. As Collins frames the argument, one compares the conditional probability of fine-tuning relative to the hypothesis of a Cosmic Designer, on the one hand, to the conditional probability of fine-tuning relative to the atheistic single universe hypothesis on the other. What probability theorists call the "likelihood" of the design hypothesis just is the conditional probability of the fine-tuning given a Designer, and the "likelihood" of the atheistic hypothesis just is the conditional probability of the fine-tuning given a single atheistic universe. Sinnott-Armstrong admits that the probability of the fine-tuning given God's existence seems high. But he fails to compare it with the probability of the fine-tuning given the atheistic single universe hypothesis. Fine-tuning is much more probable given God's existence than it is given a single atheistic universe, since in the absence of a Designer there's just no reason to expect the values of the various constants and quantities all to fall into the narrow, life-permitting range. According to a principle that probability theorists call the Likelihood Principle, the evidence of the fine-tuning of the universe therefore confirms the existence of a Cosmic Designer over the atheistic single universe hypothesis, or in other words, the hypothesis of a Cosmic Designer has a greater likelihood than the hypothesis of a single atheistic universe. Thus, fine-tuning gives us good reason to believe in the theistic hypothesis rather than in the atheistic hypothesis. Notice that the conditional probability of God's existence given the fine-tuning of the universe, mentioned by Sinnott-Armstrong, doesn't even come into play in the argument.

2. *The Many Worlds Hypothesis makes the chance hypothesis tractable.* Yes, one can so multiply one's probabilistic resources (as by postulating billions of picks in the lottery) that the odds become acceptable. But then the question is whether it is more reasonable to postulate a World Ensemble or a Designer to explain fine-tuning.

I presented four reasons why the Design Hypothesis is a better explanation than the World Ensemble Hypothesis: (1) It is simpler; (2) There is no known way for generating a randomly ordered World Ensemble; (3) There is independent evidence for the existence of God in contrast to a World Ensemble; and (4) The World Ensemble is incompatible with observations predicted by evolutionary biology.

Sinnott-Armstrong denies the greater simplicity of Design over a World Ensemble because the many postulated universes are not new types of things, as is God. But here he has confused *simplicity* with what we might call *familiarity*. The brute postulate of an indefinite collection of randomly ordered universes is definitely more complex than the postulate of a single Designer, even if universes are more familiar entities to us than are Cosmic Designers. There are various virtues of what counts as a best explanation, and I imagine familiarity is one of them.[20] But that is quite a different virtue than simplicity. In any case, the proposed hypothesis is not God as such, but intelligent design; and intelligent design is not at all an unfamiliar explanation. Thus the postulate of a Cosmic Designer is another token of the same type.

Sinnott-Armstrong's response to my remaining three objections is faltering. He tries to dismiss them as "persistent puzzles," none of which "proves God." But, of course, that's not their intended purpose. They're offered as reasons for thinking that the hypothesis of a World Ensemble is not as good an explanation as the Design Hypothesis. Nor are they mere puzzles, any more than the difficulty that undermined Boltzmann's Many Worlds Hypothesis was a mere puzzle. Notice, too, that the inference to intelligent design, whether along the lines of Dembski's statistical approach or along the lines of the probability calculus as advocated by Collins, is a *principled* inference, not "a quick fix for ignorance." Nor is it a science-stopper, as Sinnott-Armstrong alleges, since the design theorist will formulate tests to falsify his hypothesis in hopes that it will be corroborated, thereby furthering the development of rival hypotheses. Collins argues that the hypothesis of design in fact makes testable predictions, since it leads one to expect that cases of what he calls "one-sided fine-tuning," in which a constant can be shown to have an actual value very near to one edge of the life-permitting range, will turn out to involve two-sided fine-tuning, lying very near both edges of the life-permitting range. By contrast, the hypothesis of a

World Ensemble threatens to be a real science stopper if we have no way of knowing whether or not these other universes actually exist. Indeed, it's debatable whether the postulation of such a World Ensemble to dismiss the appearance of design would not undermine the scientific enterprise, since any phenomenon that appears initially puzzling can be dismissed as happening by chance alone somewhere in the infinite ensemble of worlds!

With the failure of the hypotheses of law and chance, the conclusion follows that the best explanation of the fine-tuning is design. Thus, the teleological argument nicely complements the cosmological argument.

Moral Argument

My third reason that *God Makes Sense of Objective Moral Values in the World* is a version of the moral argument for God. Sinnott-Armstrong tries to "get this argument out of the way" in section 1 of his response. Again, let's look at each of the two premises.

1. If God Does Not Exist, Objective Moral Values Do Not Exist

Sinnott-Armstrong insists that "many atheists are happy to embrace objective moral values." You bet they are! It would be hard to live without them. College sophomores may give lip service to relativism, but even they don't really live that way. Philosophers, who are more reflective, tend to recognize the objective existence of moral values and duties. The question is whether on the atheistic world view they have any *basis* for doing so or whether they simply want to enjoy the benefits of theft over honest toil. Sinnott-Armstrong makes two points in defense of objective moral values within an atheistic world view.

1. *The morality of an action is determined by whether it causes unjustified harm to another person.* This claim is, however, very problematic for the atheist. First, given atheism, why think that it is true? Why, given atheism, think that inflicting harm on other people would have any moral dimension at all? Sinnott-Armstrong rejects Atheistic Moral Realism. So why would it be wrong to hurt another member of our species? He answers, "It simply is. Objectively. Don't you agree?" Of course, I agree that it *is* wrong, since I am a theist. But I can't see any reason to think that it *would be* wrong if atheism were

true. For on atheism we are just animals, and animals don't have moral duties. Sinnott-Armstrong retorts that human beings are unlike other animals because we are "moral agents." But this claim seems to assume precisely what needs to be proved, unless some neutral content can be given to the concept of "moral agent." Sinnott-Armstrong states that moral agents "make free choices" and determine their actions by their "conception of what is moral or not." This response is ironic precisely because Sinnott-Armstrong denies that we do make free choices in the libertarian sense[21]; he believes that all our actions are determined, which leaves no room for moral agency. In any case, I see no reason to think that these conditions are sufficient, rather than merely necessary, conditions of being a moral agent. Even if we freely make decisions based on our conceptions of what is moral/immoral, the question remains whether our conceptions of what is moral/immoral have any objective validity.

Second, Sinnott-Armstrong's assertion appears to be circular. Not all harm done to other members of our species is said to be wrong, only *unjustified* harm. But what does that mean? It can't mean merely that the perpetrator has a reason for acting as he does, for murderers and rapists have such reasons and may well be pursuing their self-interest. Rather the reason must be a morally sufficient reason if it is to exonerate doing harm. But then aren't we presupposing morality in trying to ground morality? We're saying that an action is morally unjustified if it causes harm that is morally unjustified—no duh!

2. *Theism provides no better grounding of morality than atheism.* Sinnott-Armstrong recognizes that "Philosophers still might long for deeper explanations of why it is immoral for moral agents to cause unjustified harm." But, he insists, this dissatisfaction would be problematic for atheism only if the theist could provide a better explanation, which Sinnott-Armstrong denies. He thinks the Euthyphro dilemma exposes the explanatory deficiency of theism by showing that God's commands are either superfluous or arbitrary. But it seems to me that an appropriately formulated divine command morality, such as has been articulated by Adams, Quinn, Alston, and others,[22] eludes the horns of the Euthyphro dilemma by forging a third alternative: our moral duties are grounded in the commands of a holy and loving God. God's very nature is what Plato called the "Good": He is essentially kind, just, generous, and so forth. Just as

it made no sense prior to 1960 to ask whether the standard meter bar at the *Bureau de Poids et Mesures* in Paris was actually a meter long (since its length determined what a meter was), so it makes no sense to measure God's moral character against some abstract standard, since His nature is determinative of what goodness is. His nature expresses itself toward us in the form of moral commands which, issuing from the Good, become moral duties for us. Thus, God's commands are not arbitrary. If it be asked, "Why pick God's nature as constitutive of the Good?" the answer is that God, by definition, is worthy of worship and only a being that is morally perfect is so worthy. Theism thus succeeds precisely where atheism fails, in providing a metaphysical foundation for the objective existence of moral values and duties.

2. Objective Moral Values Exist

Sinnott-Armstrong agrees. His only confusion here is to think that our ability simply to see that rape is wrong implies that no account need be given of why rape is wrong. That is to confuse moral epistemology with moral ontology.

From the two premises, the conclusion that God exists follows deductively.

Resurrection of Jesus

My fourth reason is that *God Makes Sense of the Life, Death, and Resurrection of Jesus*. As Sinnott-Armstrong discerns, this is properly an argument from miracles, indeed, the central miracle of the New Testament. The form of this argument is that of an inductive inference to the best explanation of a given body of historical facts. Let's review each premise.

1. There Are Four Established Facts Concerning the Fate of Jesus of Nazareth: His Honorable Burial by Joseph of Arimathea, the Discovery of His Empty Tomb, His Post-Mortem Appearances, and the Origin of His Disciples' Belief in His Resurrection

Let's take them one at a time.

The Honorable Burial. Sinnott-Armstrong doesn't dispute this fact. Yet this fact is highly significant because it implies that the location of Jesus' gravesite would in time have become common knowledge in Jerusalem to both Jew and Christian alike.

The Empty Tomb.   Sinnott-Armstrong would rebut the evidence by asserting that *our records come from years later, during which time distortions could arise.* That's correct; but the question remains whether or to what degree such distortions *did* arise. Sinnott-Armstrong's sweeping generalization that "distortions *could* arise" does nothing either to show that the accounts of the discovery of Jesus' empty tomb are in fact unhistorical distortions or to refute the specific evidence I presented for the historical core of the narrative. The sources for Greco-Roman history are usually biased and usually one or two generations removed from the events they record, yet historians reconstruct with confidence the course of Greco-Roman history.[23] If one could really refute the specific evidence for putatively historical accounts so summarily as Sinnott-Armstrong seems to think, one might as well just close the history department at the university. In fact, most historical scholars who have examined the accounts of the empty tomb of Jesus have concluded that distorting influences have not expunged the historical core of the accounts.

The Post-Mortem Appearances.   Sinnott-Armstrong merely asks, *How do we know some witnesses did not hear stories about the others?* He misunderstands the point. Our records of the appearances are literarily independent of one another, as a comparison of them reveals. That creates a predisposition toward historicity, since multiple, independent sources concerning an event make it less likely that the event was purely legendary or invented.[24] Virtually no historian denies that the disciples had such experiences; the only question is, how are they best explained?

The Origin of the Disciples' Belief.   Sinnott-Armstrong asserts that *stories about a rising Messiah were common.* I'm afraid that he is just misinformed on this score. There was absolutely no anticipation that Messiah, when he came, would, instead of vanquishing Israel's enemies and restoring the throne of David, be shamefully executed by them.[25] And, of course, neither was there then any expectation that Messiah would be raised from the dead. Thus, the disciples' suddenly and sincerely coming to believe that Jesus was risen from the dead cannot be explained as a result of Jewish influences.

Sinnott-Armstrong's mention of Mithraism is baffling, since Mithraism does not even purport that Mithras was raised from the dead.[26] Perhaps Sinnott-Armstrong hopes to resuscitate the hypothesis of the nineteenth-century History of Religions School that myths of dying and rising pagan deities like Osiris and Adonis led the disciples to believe that Jesus rose from the dead. That hypothesis, however, collapsed early in the twentieth century due to two factors: (1) The purported parallels were spurious. These pagan deities were merely mythological symbols of the crop cycle, as vegetation dies during the dry season and comes back to life during the rainy season. Moreover, orientalists have questioned whether it is proper to speak of "resurrection" at all with regard to these deities. Observing that the idea of resurrection is late and tenuous in the case of Adonis, practically non-existent in the case of Attis, and inapplicable in the case of Osiris, who merely lives on in the Underworld, M. S. Smith concludes, "it is presently impossible to accept a general category of a 'dying and rising god' in the ancient Mediterranean and Levantine world."[27] (2) The causal connection is missing. As the eminent New Testament historian Martin Hengel explains, it was precisely because of Jewish belief in the resurrection of the dead that the Hellenistic mystery religions "could gain virtually no influence" in Jewish Palestine.[28] Thus, even the sceptical critic Hans Grass admits that it would have been "completely unthinkable" for the Jewish disciples of Jesus to have sincerely come to believe that Jesus was risen from the dead because of the influence of myths of pagan deities.[29]

We therefore have good grounds for the four facts that serve as our inductive data base. It's worth emphasizing that these facts, while by no means universally acknowledged, are accepted today by most New Testament historians who have written on the subject.

2. The Hypothesis "God Raised Jesus from the Dead" Is the Best Explanation of these Facts

Sinnott-Armstrong raises two objections:

1. *Someone stole the body.* Notice that apart from his unsubstantiated assertion that "many people had motive and opportunity to

move the body," Sinnott-Armstrong provides no evidence for this hypothesis. It thus has no more probability than what it acquires from our general background knowledge. On the other hand, against it stands the following specific evidence: (1) No one had a motive to steal the body. Grave robbers are after the goods interred with the body, such as jewelry, not the corpse itself. In imagining other persons with a motive, I suspect that Sinnott-Armstrong is thinking anachronistically in terms of someone's faking the resurrection. (2) No party can be plausibly thought to have removed the body of Jesus from the tomb. Not the disciples, for their sincerity was evident in their willingness to die for their belief that Jesus had been raised; not the authorities, for they would have produced the body once the disciples began to preach the resurrection; not ordinary Jews, for there was just no reason to do such a thing. There just isn't anybody who can be identified as the alleged perpetrators. (3) No one apart from Joseph of Arimathea (and anyone with him) and the women even knew immediately following the crucifixion where the body of Jesus was laid. Joseph must have surprised everyone when he gave Jesus an honorable burial rather than allowing the Romans to dispatch the corpse in the customary manner. (4) The time was too short for such a plot to be hatched and executed. Jesus was unexpectedly given an honorable burial late Friday afternoon; by dawn on Sunday the body was gone. The window of opportunity for coming up with such an idea, assembling the people required, and carrying out the theft is so narrow as to militate against such an explanation. (5) The theft would have eventually come to light. Such conspiracies inevitably unravel, and the Jewish authorities, who had bought off Judas to betray Jesus, would have paid handsomely for any information concerning a theft of Jesus' corpse. Instead we find the earliest Jewish polemic lamely charging that the disciples themselves had stolen Jesus' body (Matthew 28.13). (6) The grave clothes left in the tomb (Luke 24.12; John 20.7) show that the tomb had not been emptied by robbery. Tomb robbers would not undress and unbind the corpse and carry it off naked, with limbs dangling, leaving the wrappings behind. (7) The theft hypothesis has deficient explanatory scope. It aims to explain the empty tomb but says nothing about the resurrection appearances or the origin of the disciples' belief in Jesus' resurrection (which an empty tomb alone cannot account for). Thus, the theory is multiply flawed.

2. *The resurrection hypothesis contradicts all the evidence for the laws of nature violated by it.* This is the *real* reason Sinnott-Armstrong prefers the theft hypothesis, despite its want of positive evidence and its many deficiencies! But this objection is merely a reprise of Hume's fallacious and oft-refuted argument against the identification of miracles.[30] The evidence for the laws of nature counts against the hypothesis that Jesus rose *naturally* from the dead (virtually any hypothesis is more plausible than that!), but it doesn't count against the hypothesis "God raised Jesus from the dead." Moreover, probability theory requires that we also consider the probability of our having the evidence for the empty tomb, resurrection appearances, and the origin of the disciples' belief if Jesus had *not* risen from the dead, which might strike us as very low. Sinnott-Armstrong is correct that the resurrection hypothesis is ad hoc, in the sense of postulating an additional entity, God. But his own theory is also ad hoc in postulating without evidence conspirators who stole Jesus' body. In any case, the ad hoc-ness of the resurrection hypothesis can be outweighed by its greater explanatory power, scope, and plausibility. The religio-historical context in which the resurrection occurred (Jesus' unparalleled life and radical claims) makes it utterly unlike Sinnott-Armstrong's fanciful ice cream illustration. Moreover, the resurrection hypothesis is part of a cumulative case for theism, which includes several other independent reasons to think that God exists.

Apart from an unjustified prejudice against miracles, I think that it's hard to deny that the resurrection hypothesis is the best explanation of the evidence.

Immediate Experience of God

My fifth reason is that *God Can Be Immediately Known and Experienced*. Sinnott-Armstrong replies to this reason in section 3 of his chapter.

Sinnott-Armstrong objects that *the diversity of religious claims undermines the reliability of religious experience.* But he didn't reply to my answer to this anticipated objection.[31] Unless I have some reason to think that my experience of the inner witness of God's Spirit is delusory, the mere presence of other persons claiming a similar experience in support of counter-Christian claims does not in itself serve to make my belief improper. Moreover, the objection assumes that all religious experiences "seem similar from the inside." That assumption is false, as an examination of the variety of religious experiences reveals. The Hindu experience of one's subsumption in the Whole is a very different experience from Christian experience of God's love. The veridicality of Christian experience thus need not imply that other types of religious experience are not genuine apprehensions of God in certain aspects of His being.

What makes belief in God basic for some person is the fact that this person holds it without founding it on arguments or other beliefs, and what makes it properly basic for him is that it is not held arbitrarily but is grounded in his experience. That experience need not be so overwhelming that he would be crazy not to hold the belief in question; indeed, most properly basic beliefs (like one's memory belief of what one had for lunch yesterday) are not of such a quality. Thus, my claim is not that atheists are crazy but that one who has an immediate experience of God, such as the Bible promises to those who sincerely seek Him, may know, in the absence of any defeaters, in a properly basic way that God exists.

In any case, the independent confirmation demanded by Sinnott-Armstrong is available for belief in the existence of the biblical God, as our previous four arguments show. But even in their absence, a person can be warranted in holding theistic belief in a properly basic way, even if others appeal to similar experiences to ground their incompatible beliefs in a basic way.

In summary, it seems to me that all five of my reasons to think that God exists survive Sinnott-Armstrong's criticisms. Unless he can, then, provide sound, equally plausible arguments for atheism, the preponderance of the evidence favors theism, and the rational person will find in theism reason enough to merit his joyful assent.

Notes

1. Thus, insofar as the God of the Bible is omnipotent and omniscient, our cumulative case has justified our believing God to have even those properties.

2. Wesley C. Salmon, *Logic*, Foundations of Philosophy Series (Englewood Cliffs, N.J.: Prentice-Hall, 1963), 63. (How's that for an appeal to authority!)

3. Ibid., 64.

4. R. T. France, "The Gospels at Historical Sources for Jesus, the Founder of Christianity," *Truth* 1 (1985): 86. As examples, France mentions A. N. Sherwin-White, *Roman Society and Roman Law in the New Testament* (Oxford: Oxford University Press, 1963), 186–192, and A. T. Hanson, ed., *Vindications* (London: SCM, 1966), 42–43, 94–95.

5. For an elementary account of some of the options, see Nick Herbert's delightful book, *Quantum Reality: Beyond the New Physics* (Garden City, N.Y.: Doubleday Anchor Press, 1985). Further interpretations have appeared since he wrote.

6. Bernulf Kanitscheider, "Does Physical Cosmology Transcend the Limits of Naturalistic Reasoning?" in *Studies on Mario Bunge's "Treatise*," ed. P. Weingartner and G. J. W. Dorn (Amsterdam: Rodopi, 1990), 346–347.

7. Edward Kasner and James Newman, *Mathematics and the Imagination* (New York: Simon & Schuster, 1940), 61. For example, Alexander Abian interprets existence in set theory to mean merely that certain specified sets will be listed in an illusory table describing the theory of sets (see Alexander Abian, *The Theory of Sets and Transfinite Arithmetic* [Philadelphia: W. B. Saunders, 1965] 68).

8. Sinnott-Armstrong misleads in saying that Hilbert recognized that "his finitist project was undermined by Gödel's incompleteness theorems." What Gödel's theorems undermined was Hilbert's Formalist program of trying to prove the consistency of arithmetic in a finite number of steps. Nothing in Gödel's theorems compels us to believe that actual infinites exist.

9. Actually, it is Sinnott-Armstrong's interpretation of the physics that seems questionable. For example, the reason most physicists don't like an initial cosmological singularity has virtually nothing to do with "doubts that gravity is always attractive," as he claims, but because a singularity represents the breakdown of physics and so the terminus of science, an undesirable state of affairs for a scientist! It is the prospect of the initial singularity that has helped to drive the quest for alternative models. But even non-singular models like the Hartle-Hawking model still involve an absolute, if non-singular, beginning.

10. He has reference to an article by James Glanz, "Tiniest of Particles Pokes Big Hole in Physics Theory," *New York Times* (Feb 8, 2001), pp. A1, A21, concerning the possible detection at Brookhaven National Laboratory of a precession in the motion of certain elementary particles. Let me explain. The precession counts in favor of a theory of elementary particle physics called supersymmetry. According to the Standard Model of particle physics, fundamen-

tal particles are classed as either fermions (particles that make up matter) or bosons (particles that carry the four forces of nature). Fermions include quarks (which are the constituents of particles like protons and neutrons) and leptons (simple particles like electrons and neutrinos). Bosons include photons (which carry the electromagnetic force), gravitons (which carry the gravitational force), gluons (which carry the weak force), and intermediate vector bosons (which transmit the weak force). Many physicists find this model "ugly" because it lacks a unifying symmetry and is unwieldy. Various strategies for unifying these particles and forces are being explored. So-called Grand Unified Theories (GUTs) would unite the strong, weak, and electromagnetic forces at very high energy levels such as prevailed in the first split-second after the Big Bang into one Grand Unified force carried by hypothetical X and Y particles. Under such theories, quarks and leptons become at the same time interconvertible. Supersymmetry (SUSY) is an attempt to achieve further unification by incorporating gravitation into the GUT. In order to make fermions and bosons fully interchangeable, they must be put into symmetrical pairings. SUSY would achieve this by postulating new particles like squarks and sleptons for fermions, and like photinos, gravitinos, gluinos, etc., for bosons. The Brookhaven results are the first empirical evidence in favor of SUSY, since the precession seems to suggest the existence of a yet undiscovered particle. Such discoveries were anticipated and fully consonant with standard Big Bang cosmology. In general we'd do well to reflect on the words of the Astronomer Royal Martin Rees, "Cosmological ideas are no longer any more fragile and evanescent than our theories about the history of our Earth. . . . The empirical support for a Big Bang ten to fifteen billion years ago is as compelling as the evidence that geologists offer on our Earth's history" (*Just Six Numbers* [New York: Basic Books, 2000], 10).

11. John Barrow and Frank Tipler, *The Anthropic Cosmological Principle* (Oxford: Clarendon Press, 1986), 442.

12. See my "The Ultimate Question of Origins: God and the Beginning of the Universe," *Astrophysics and Space Science* 269–270 (1999): 723–740, or my "Naturalism and Cosmology," in *Naturalism: A Critical Analysis*, ed. Wm. L. Craig and J. P. Moreland, Routledge Studies in Twentieth-Century Philosophy, (London: Routledge, 2000), 215–252. At the time of this writing all the buzz is Paul Steinhardt's new cyclical model of the origin of the universe (see http://feynman.princeton.edu/~steinh/) based upon the periodic collision of three-dimensional membranes. It will be very interesting to see how well this new model fares under criticism! See Gary Felder, Andret Frolov, Lev Kofman, and Andrei Linde, "Cosmology with Negative Potentials," http://arXiv.org/abs/hep-th/0202017 (16 February 2002) and the therein cited literature; Arvind Borde, Alan Guth, and Alexander Vilenkin, "Inflation Is Not Past-Eternal," http://arXiv:gr-qc/0110012v1 (1 Oct 2001).

13. Christopher Isham, "Space, Time, and Quantum Cosmology." Paper presented at the conference "God, Time, and Modern Physics," March 1990; idem, "Quantum Cosmology and the Origin of the Universe." Lecture presented at the conference "Cosmos and Creation," Cambridge University, 14 July 1994.

14. Someone might say that if the fundamental quantities were radically varied perhaps forms of life as yet unimagined might have energed. It's hard to see how any life at all could be possible in a world in which not even chemistry could exist; but let that pass. The more important point is that we need not consider such radically different worlds, but only those in our neighborhood. Imagine a fly resting in a large blank area of the wall. A single shot is fired, and the bullet pierces the fly. It is reasonable to conclude the shot was aimed, even if the wall outside the local area is covered with flies so that a randomly fired shot would strike one. Similarly, within our local area of possible universes, life-permitting universes are incomprehensibly rare, even if wildly different universes might permit some other form of life. (The fly illustration is John Leslie's.)

15. I'm indebted to an excellent discussion of this question by Robin Collins, "Fine-Tuning and Comparison Range." In press. Be on the lookout for his forthcoming book *The Well-Tempered Universe,* a *tour de force* on the problem of fine-tuning and design inference. Collins specifically addresses the concerns raised in the article by the McGrews and Vestrup, cited in Sinnott-Armstrong's note 12.

16. These examples are discussed at length by Robin Collins, "Evidence for Fine-Tuning" in press.

17. Lawrence Krauss, "Cosmological Antigravity," *Scientific American* (January 1999): 59; V. Sahni and A. Starobinsky, "The Case for a Positive Cosmological Lambda-Term," (28 April 1999); available online at http://xxx.lanl.gov/abs/astro-ph/9904398. I'm indebted to Collins, "Evidence for Fine-Tuning," for these references.

18. Collins, "Evidence for Fine-Tuning."

19. Ibid. The quotation is from B. J. Carr and M. J. Rees, "The Anthropic Cosmological Principle and the Structure of the Physical World," *Nature* 278 (12 April 1979): 612.

20. In their book *A Subject with No Object* (Oxford: Clarendon Press, 1997), 209, John P. Burgess and Gideon Rosen list seven features that tend to be used in guiding scientific theory choice. Among them are both minimality (or economy) of assumptions and coherence with familiar, established theories.

21. He makes this clear in our debate "Do Evil and Suffering Disprove God?" (April 2, 2000), Wooddale Church, Eden Prairie, Minn.

22. Philip L. Quinn, *Divine Commands and Moral Requirements* (Oxford: Clarendon Press, 1978); Robert Merrihew Adams, *Finite and Infinite Goods* (Oxford: Oxford University Press, 2000); William Alston, "What Euthyphro Should Have Said," in *Philosophy of Religion: A Reader and Guide*, ed. Wm. L. Craig (Edinburgh: Edinburgh University Press, 2001; New Brunswick, N.J.: Rutgers University Press, 2001), 283–298.

23. See A. N. Sherwin White, *Roman Society and Roman Law in the New Testament* (Oxford: Clarendon Press, 1963), 186–191.

24. On the importance of early, multiple attestation, see Marcus Borg, "Seeing Jesus: Sources, Lenses, and Methods," in *The Meaning of Jesus*, by Marcus Borg and N. T. Wright (San Francisco: HarperCollins, 1999), 12.

25. A point emphasized by N. T. Wright, "The Crux of Faith," in *The Meaning of Jesus*, by Marcus Borg and N. T. Wright (San Francisco: HarperCollins, 1999), 102, 117–118.

26. For a nice popular account see Ronald Nash, *Christianity and the Hellenistic World* (Grand Rapids, Mich.: Zondervan, 1984), 143–148, 169–173.

27. Mark S. Smith, *The Ugaritic Baal Cycle*, Vol. I. (Leiden: E. J. Brill, 1994), 70.

28. Martin Hengel, *Judenthum und Hellenismus*, WUNT 10 (Tübingen: J. C. B. Mohr, 1969), 368–369.

29. Hans Grass, *Ostergeschehen und Osterberichte*, 4th ed. (Göttingen: Vandenhoeck & Ruprecht, 1970), 133.

30. For a recent, devastating critique by a prominent philosopher of science, who is himself an agnostic, see John Earman, *Hume's Abject Failure* (Oxford: Oxford University Press, 2000). See further, George Campbell, *Dissertation on Miracles* (1762; rep. ed.: London: T. Tegg & Son, 1834); Gottfried Less, *Wahrheit der christlichen Religion* (Göttingen: G. L. Förster, 1776); William Paley, *A View of the Evidence of Christianity*, 5th ed. 2 vols. (London: R. Faulder, 1796; reprint ed.: Westmead, UK: Gregg, 1970); Richard Swinburne, *The Concept of Miracle* (New York: Macmillan, 1970); John Earman, "Bayes, Hume, and Miracles," *Faith and Philosophy* 10 (1993): 293–310; George Mavrodes, "Miracles and the Laws of Nature," *Faith and Philosophy* 2 (1985): 333–346; William Alston, "God's Action in the World," in *Divine Nature and Human Language* (Ithaca, NY: Cornell University Press, 1989), 197–222.

31. See pp. 27–28.

PART 2

CHAPTER 4

Some Reasons to Believe that There Is No God

Walter Sinnott-Armstrong

In the first part of this book, I criticized Craig's arguments for the existence of God, but criticism goes only so far. Even if there is no decent argument *for* the existence of God, there also might not be any decent argument *against* the existence of God. Consequently, my criticisms are compatible with *agnosticism*, which is the view that we cannot know whether or not God exists. In this section, I will go further and present positive arguments for *atheism*, which is the view that God does not exist.

Why would anyone argue against the existence of God? If you feel sure that God does not exist, why come out of the closet and announce your reasons publicly? You are bound to make enemies. You won't convince anybody. Why bother? Many friends have asked me these questions. They deserve an answer.

My answer is that I am a teacher, so my job is to educate. I am also a philosopher. Philosophers question common assumptions and inspect the reasons for and against those assumptions. That is why I want to help readers get clear about the evidence for and against the existence of God, so that they can decide for themselves. If you look at the evidence with an open mind, then you will conclude that God does not exist, or so I believe. But even if you do not reach this conclusion, if you do achieve a better understanding of the evidence on both sides, then I will have achieved my main purpose.

My goal is not to undermine religion. Some atheists want to subvert religion, because they see religion as the source of many social and personal problems. They have a point. Many wars in the past and today result (in part) from religious differences. Witness the Crusades long ago and the current conflicts in Ireland and the Middle East. Many fine people have been executed, tortured, tormented, and ostracized in the name of religion. Witness not only the Inquisition but also Matthew Shepard, who was tortured and killed because of his harmless sexual proclivities. Many more people suffer because religious institutions resist certain advances in education, culture, and medicine. Witness stem cell research, which promises to cure juvenile diabetes along with other horrors; its funding is restricted by the United States government because of opposition by religious leaders (and almost nobody else). So religious belief is costly. Those costs are what motivate some atheists to argue against the existence of God.

I share many of these concerns, but they are not my reasons for arguing that there is no God. In my view, religion is not all bad. Faith leads many people to perform wonderful acts of charity that they might not perform if they did not have faith. Faith can bind families and communities together in mutually beneficial ways. Some people need faith to face difficulties and find meaning and hope in their lives. Like law, science, art, and guns, religion is a powerful tool that can be used for great good as well as for great evil. I have no desire to obstruct the benefits of religion.

Luckily, the truth will not hurt us. Religion can play its positive roles without all of the fancy doctrines that theologians construct. Most religious believers love the songs, stories, rituals, communities, and moral teachings of their religions. They do not understand or care much about obscure details of theology. Indeed, many people would come to doubt their religion if they thought through the extreme theories of theologians. Dubious doctrines, no matter how popular, weaken religion by making it more questionable. So the faithful should not worry about reconsidering dubious doctrines. They should welcome this enterprise with an open mind.

One particular collection of doctrines will be my target here. These doctrines are not common to all religions. They are not accepted by Hindus or Buddhists, or even by all Jews or Christians. According to many historians, this collection of doctrines was not put together until the early Middle Ages, so it is not part of early Judaism or early Christianity, including the New Testament. This historical claim might be questioned, and some Christians might insist that these doctrines are essential to true Christianity. Still, many other people who call themselves Christians reject these doctrines, at least in the versions that cause trouble. Anyway, I take no stand on what counts as true Christianity. Whenever they got started, these doctrines became central to later Judaism and to Islam, as well as to many currently popular versions of Christianity. That is what makes it worthwhile to question them here.

What are these dubious doctrines? According to traditional (even if not original) Christianity, God is defined to be:

- All-good (= God always does the best that He can)
- All-powerful (= God can do anything that is logically possible)
- All-knowing (= God knows everything that is true)
- Eternal (= God exists outside of time)
- Effective (= God causes changes in time)
- Personal (= God has a will and makes choices)

From now on, when I refer to God, I will mean a being with these defining features. When I argue against the existence of God, I will be arguing that nothing has all of these features.

My arguments will not be proofs in the mathematical sense. I don't see how there could be any absolutely conclusive proof of any view about God, either that He does exist or that He does not exist. There is not much, if anything, of importance that one can prove with certainty beyond any doubt whatsoever. So I won't even try to give a conclusive proof. What I will give is adequate evidence against the existence of God. That is enough to justify the belief that God does not exist.

This evidence comes in the form of three arguments (although more could be given). None of these arguments is original. Still, they are worth repeating, because many people do not fully appreciate their force.

1. The Problem of Evil

My first argument focuses on the first three defining features of God. It is very common and simple: There is lots of evil in the world.

There would not be so much evil if there were an all-good and all-powerful God. Therefore, there is no such God.

In its most powerful form, this argument focuses on examples like this: Many babies each year are born with Down's syndrome. Most of these babies, with normal pediatric care, will grow up healthy. A significant number, however, have intestinal obstructions that will kill them if they do not receive an operation. Without the operation, dehydration and infection will cause these babies to wither and die over a period of hours and days. Today this operation is relatively simple, but not long ago these babies could not be saved. So just think about a baby born with Down's syndrome and an intestinal blockage in 1900. This baby suffers for days, then dies. If the details of this example are doubted, or if one example does not seem to be enough, then I could describe many more birth defects and diseases that cause babies excruciating pain and death after only very short lives. There is no shortage of horror.

To complete the example, suppose a doctor could have cured the child and enabled it to live a happy life with a simple operation that would not cost much to anybody. Nonetheless, the doctor chose not to save the child. Why not? Imagine that the doctor just did not feel like operating that day. I would consider this doctor to be a moral monster. I assume that most of you would agree. If the doctor can save the child with little cost to anyone, but the doctor chooses to let it die, then the doctor cannot be a good person, to say the least.

Now apply these standards to God. In the traditional conception, God is all-powerful, so He could have saved the child easily. All He had to do was remove the intestinal obstruction. Doctors can do that, so God can, too. Better yet, God could help the baby secretly and painlessly by changing the child's genes so that this baby would never have had Down's syndrome or, at least, an intestinal blockage. God's cure need not harm anyone else. The doctor might need the operating table for another patient, but God's mercy would not use up any medical resources. The doctor might be too busy, but not God. A doctor might worry that the child or the child's parents will suffer more later, but God could prevent that future suffering as well. All of this might take a miracle, but there is nothing logically impossible about God helping this baby with no harm to anyone, so God can do it.

Given these alternatives, did God have an adequate reason to let this baby suffer and die? I cannot see any. I bet you can't either. If God did have some reason to let this baby suffer and die, He could tell us His reason, and He would have no adequate reason not to tell us. Thus, since we see no adequate reason for it, this baby's suffering is evidence that there is no God who has all of the features in the traditional conception.

Notice that each bit of unjustified evil is evidence against God, according to this argument. If I claimed to be all-good, one bad act would refute me. If I claimed to be all-powerful, you could disprove this claim by finding one thing that I cannot lift. Similarly, even one bit of unjustified evil disproves the existence of God. Still, it is worth adding that there is *lots* of evil in the world. Many children through the centuries have been born with intestinal blockages. There are many more kinds of birth defects that lead to short lives filled with intense suffering. Every day many children die from disease or malnutrition. The world includes floods, hurricanes, tornadoes, volcanoes, earthquakes, lightning, and many other natural disasters. Children and adults get trapped under rubble and then die after hours of horrible suffering. Take any individual natural disaster. An all-powerful God could prevent this natural disaster from occurring. He could do so without harming people as much as they are harmed by the natural disaster. So there seems to be no adequate reason why He should let these natural disasters occur. That means that God would not let them occur if He were all-good. But they do occur. So there is ample evidence against the existence of any all-powerful, all-good God.

That's the basic idea, but my argument can be presented more formally and generally like this:

1. If there were an all-powerful and all-good God, then there would not be any evil in the world unless that evil is logically necessary for an adequately compensating good.
2. There is lots of evil in the world.
3. Much of that evil is not logically necessary for any adequately compensating good.
4. Therefore, there is no God who is all-powerful and all-good.

Arguments like this are sometimes said to show that evil is logically inconsistent with an all-good and all-powerful God. I do not claim that much here. The point of my argument is, instead, that evil is evidence against the existence of an all-good and all-powerful God, at least when that evil is not logically necessary for any adequately compensating good. Thus, my argument is a version of what is called "the evidential argument from evil" rather than "the logical argument from evil."

This argument depends on the notion of evil, which needs to be explained. When you call people evil, you probably think that their motives and characters are morally bad. In contrast, I will use the term "evil" more broadly to include anything that is harmful or bad, even if no moral agent causes it or could prevent it. In this wide sense, there are many disagreements about what is evil, but I need not settle them here. The only examples that I need are obvious. Under "evil," I include intense pain (or suffering), serious disabilities (mental and physical), and death. There are probably also other evils. I do not deny, for example, that unfairness and injustice (both distributive and retributive) are evils. Thus, I do not assume any crude form of utilitarianism. The reason why I focus on pain, disability, and death is only that there are plenty of these evils for my argument, and there is less question that they are evils. The other evils are harder to identify and more questionable, so I will not use them in my argument. In fact, I don't even need all of the items on my list of evils. Even if one item on my list is questioned, the others should be enough. But it does strike me and almost everyone else as obvious that pain, disabilities, and death are evils.

What makes these things evil? That is a tough question that I do not need to answer here. It is enough for my argument that these things are evil, even if it is not clear what makes them evil or what it means to call them evil. Still, if you demand a general account of evil, my colleague Bernard Gert plausibly identifies an evil as anything that all rational people avoid for themselves unless they have an adequate reason to want it. Pain, disability, and death are evils because anyone who fails to avoid them without an adequate reason is, to that extent, irrational.

Of course, we often do have an adequate reason to accept pain, disability, and even death. I pay my dentist to drill my teeth in very painful ways. Is this crazy? It would be, if the drilling did not serve any purpose; but a trip to the dentist is not irrational because the dentist prevents more pain in the future.

When is an evil justified? Only when it is necessary to gain some good or to prevent some evil. If I could prevent tooth decay with an innocuous pill rather than by paying a dentist to drill my teeth, it would normally be stupid to choose the drill over the pill. Moreover, not every reason is adequate. Even though leg cramps are painful, and even if there is no other way to prevent periodic leg cramps except by cutting off someone's legs, the pain of leg cramps is still not an adequate reason to cut off that person's legs. There are disagreements about which reasons are adequate, but some cases are clear, and everyone recognizes some reasons as inadequate. In any case, evils can be justified only by benefits that are adequate to compensate for those evils. This is just common sense about what is rational.

Morality enters the story when evil is caused not just to oneself but to other people. (Morality might also restrict some harms to oneself and to lower animals, but we can avoid those controversial issues here.) It is morally wrong to cause evils to other people, although again we have to add "unless one has an adequate reason."

Morally, we also should not fail to prevent important harms to others when we can easily prevent those harms at little or no cost to anyone, including ourselves. A common example is a baby who crawls into a pool and starts to drown. If I can save this baby's life at no cost other than my getting wet, then it would be immoral for me to walk away and let it drown. Maybe I shouldn't save it when somehow I know that it will grow up to become a mass murderer. Maybe I don't have to save it when other people can and will save it if I don't. Maybe I have an excuse when saving it would be dangerous or when there are too many drowning babies for me to save them all. Moralists disagree about how far anyone needs to go to prevent harm to others. It is not controversial, however, that we should prevent serious harm when nobody else can or will prevent it and we can easily and safely prevent it and similar harms with no significant cost to anyone.

Controversy arises when there are significant costs in preventing an evil or gaining a benefit. Still, a few general points seem clear. As in the case of dentists, to be adequate as compensation for an evil, the compensating benefit must be important enough, and there must be no better way to prevent the evil. When other people are

affected, it also must not be unfair to cause or allow the evil in order to gain the benefit. For example, a doctor would not be justified in taking one person's liver without consent to transplant into
another person, even if that other person would die without the liver.
The death of the unwilling organ donor is an evil, and the other person's life is an important compensation. Still, this compensation is
not adequate morally, because it is unfair to sacrifice one person to
save another without consent (other things being equal). This restriction on fairness in compensation shows, again, that I do not assume any crude utilitarianism.

This little bit of moral theory is common sense that can be accepted by those who believe in God, as well as those who do not.
This moral common ground is worth highlighting here, because atheists are often accused of being amoral or immoral. This accusation
has no basis. Atheists can, and often do, accept very stringent moral
principles that restrict not only causing harm but also failing to prevent harm. The moral principles of atheists need not be any different from the moral principles of theists (except on religious issues,
such as blasphemy).

The problem of evil arises when we apply these common moral
principles to God. God is supposed to be more skilled than any human. God can save drowning babies without even getting wet. God
can prevent tooth decay with no pain at all. It might seem that even
God cannot do this, because tooth decay results from laws of nature.
But God is supposed to be able to perform miracles. God can intervene in nature and even change the laws of nature. This follows
from the definition of God as all-powerful in the sense that He can
do anything that is logically possible. The only evils that such a God
cannot avoid without loss are those that it is logically impossible to
avoid without loss. Consequently, the only evils that God is justified
in allowing are those that are logically necessary to promote some
adequately compensating good. That explains why I used the term
"logically necessary" in my premises.

As I said, my argument is very old. Over the centuries, many
Christians have responded to it, but no response is adequate, or so
I will try to show. I cannot consider every possible response, but I
will quickly survey the most prominent responses. The first two responses question premise (2). The next six responses deny premise

(3). The last three responses raise broader issues about method. Some of these responses are rarely used today, but they are still worth running through to cover the territory.

The Unconscious Response: Maybe there is no evil in the world, since, for example, the babies who seem to suffer might not be conscious, in which case they never really feel any pain.

Criticism: Nobody could believe this while they watch these poor babies squirm. It is possible that God anesthetizes such babies and then makes them squirm as a spectacle for us. But why would God do that? Moreover, anesthesia cannot remove the evils of disability and death. It is still logically possible that no evils occur, since even disability and death might be illusions, but that abstract possibility cannot keep our experiences from being strong evidence that there is much pain and disability and death in this world.

The Privation Response: Although pain, disability, and death occur, evil does not exist in reality, because evil is merely the privation of good, just as darkness is the absence of light.

Criticism: Anybody who has ever stubbed a toe or given birth knows that pain hurts. It is a positive sensation and not just the absence of pleasure. People who are numb or asleep do not feel pain, even though they experience the absence of pleasure and any other feeling. So pain is not a privation. More importantly, even if pain, disability, and death were all just privations, that would not make them any less evil or any less real. It would be a sick joke to try to comfort parents whose child just died by saying that their child is not really dead but merely deprived of life. Whether or not evils are privations, they should be avoided when there is no compensating good, so no metaphysical doctrine about privation can explain why God would let them occur.

The Contrast Response: If the whole world were black, we would not be aware that it is black. For that awareness, we need some other color to contrast with the black. Analogously, if there were no evil in the world, we would not be aware of the good. God then allows evil to make us aware of goodness, since this awareness is itself a good.

Criticism: To make us aware of blackness, all we need is to see a speck of white. To make us aware of goodness, all we need is to see a speck of evil. One stubbed toe is enough, or maybe one stubbed toe per person. There is far too much evil in this world for it all to be necessary to enable us to conceive of goodness. Some theists might claim that we need more evil around us in order to appreciate how good our lives are. Even if so, this is hardly laudable, and it is not logically necessary that our minds work this way, so God could make us better.

The Punishment Response: God lets people suffer because of sins for which their suffering is just retribution.

Criticism: Even babies suffer, but babies have not sinned, since they are not morally responsible yet, so there is nothing to punish them for. That is why I used babies in my examples.

Some theologians respond that God punishes babies for original sin. Adam and Eve sinned in the Garden of Eden. Babies pay now. But that would be grossly unfair. Long ago, governments did punish whole families and other groups for crimes by one member, so then the punishment response might have seemed plausible by analogy. Today, however, almost everyone agrees that group punishment is barbaric. You should not be punished for what your father or your state's governor did, especially if they did it before you were born. Why not? Because their acts were beyond your control, and it is unfair to punish people for what they cannot control. This widely accepted principle of justice would be violated by punishing babies for original sin.

God is supposed to be unlike humans who punish, since God knows the future. Maybe God punishes babies in advance for sins that they will commit if they live. But that still seems grossly unfair. If people have free will, as most traditional theists assume, that makes it unfair to punish them in advance, while they still have a chance to choose not to sin. Besides, babies with Down's syndrome are not likely to become such bad sinners that they deserve to die painfully before they sin. It is logically possible that every baby who suffers and dies would have become a mass murderer, but we have no evidence at all for such speculation. It is just as likely that these babies would have become heroes. Our evidence, thus, suggests that the evils of this world are not always distributed according to past or future sins, so these evils cannot be justified as punishment.

The Heavenly Response: Even if sinless babies suffer, they are compensated many times over by being given eternal life.

Criticism: God could send the babies straight up to heaven before they suffer. Because this option is available, their suffering is not logically necessary for them to get to heaven, so heaven cannot justify their suffering. To see why, compare a father who beats his daughter and then gives her a gift to make up for it. The beating is still immoral even if the gift is so good that she would rather have both the beating and the gift than neither. Why? Because he could have given her the gift *without* the beating. That would be better for her than both together and also better than neither. Similarly, if God lets babies suffer and then sends them to heaven for eternity, they are better off than if they had neither the suffering nor heaven. But that cannot make it right to let them suffer, since God could have sent them straight to heaven *without* the suffering. He could have caused the mother of the Down's syndrome child to miscarry, so that the baby would never have been born, would never have suffered, and would have lived only in heaven. Why didn't God choose that option? Heaven cannot answer this question.

The Virtuous Response: Evil builds good character. The child's *what!* suffering enables the parents to become more courageous and observers to become more compassionate. These and other moral virtues compensate for the evil.

Criticism: Education should be effective, efficient, and fair. Letting babies suffer and die is often a very *ineffective* way to teach courage and compassion. For one thing, suffering and death sometimes occur in secret. If nobody lives to tell the story about a suffering baby, nobody can learn from it. Even when evils are known, many observers become hardened and cynical, or despondent and isolated, rather than morally virtuous. And even when evil does teach some courage and compassion, greater losses often occur. The child's parents break up, neglect their other children, and turn away from God. If a schoolteacher used techniques this harmful, you would immediately fire that teacher. And God would know exactly which people would react well to evils. So it is hard to imagine any reason why God would adopt such a crude teaching technique in the cases where He knows that it won't be effective.

Moreover, when a lesson is expensive, it is *inefficient* to repeat it more often than is necessary. Surely God can create moral virtues with less harms than we experience. One starving or deformed child should be enough to create compassion, if the news spreads. We don't need millions.

Most importantly, even if the parents or others did become better off as a result of the baby's suffering, it would still be *unfair* to let the baby suffer in order to help those separate individuals. Compare a neighbor whose baby is suffering horribly from disease. The neighbor can help easily, but the suffering of this baby will teach a valuable lesson to his other children and to himself, so he lets the suffering continue unabated. This neighbor is a moral monster. Don't you agree? But this neighbor is analogous to God if God lets babies suffer just to build moral virtues in other people, especially since God has more and better options than any human neighbor has.

The Glorious Response: Craig sometimes says that God uses evil to maximize the number of people who know, glorify, and gain salvation from God. God's purpose is not to make humans happy but, rather, to make them glorify Him.

Criticism: This would be horribly unfair to those babies. If a father told us that he doesn't care whether his children are happy as long as they know how powerful he is and glorify him, we would think that this father is an egomaniac. God might have purposes other than making us happy, and one of his purposes might be to make us glorify Him, but our happiness can still be among His purposes. If God doesn't care at all about whether we are happy, then He is not good by our standards or in any sense that matters to us. Moreover, an all-powerful God can surely find some more effective and efficient way to lead people to glorify Him, since evil so often turns people away from God.

The Free Will Response: You wouldn't want a robot for a child, even if the robot always obeyed you, right? So you must admit that freedom is worth the price of much misbehavior. This value also justifies God in giving us free will, even though He knew that we would often misuse our free will and choose or cause evil.

Criticism: I do not deny that people have free will, although it is surprisingly hard to say what free will is. I also do not deny that free will is very valuable, although it is again hard to say why. Of course, I would never trade my children for robots, even though they do (rarely!) misbehave. What I do deny is that all evil can be justified by the value of freedom or free will.

Although I want my son to have free will, I would stop him from killing his sister. If I didn't, then I would be guilty of a serious crime. So why doesn't God stop people from killing each other? At least, why doesn't he stop *most* of them? There is way too much killing in the world to think that an all-good God could stop it but chooses to sit idly by just in order to protect the free will of murderers.

Moreover, many murderers can be stopped *without* robbing them of their free will at all. Consider a pedophile who contacts young children on the Internet, talks them into meeting him, then kidnaps them, rapes them, and kills them. Let's call one victim Mary. What would God have to do to save Mary? Just make this pedophile's computer crash right before he contacts Mary. The pedophile would still have free will, but he would not cause as much pain and suffering. So why doesn't God foil evil plans or turn evil people into klutzes?

Finally, even if the value of free will did explain why God allows evil that is caused by humans, it still would *not* explain why God allows *natural* evil. Natural evil is evil that arises independently of human actions. It includes most of the pain, anguish, and loss of life that is caused by lightning and earthquakes and diseases and so on. The free will defense does not apply to natural evil. Diseases, birth defects, tornadoes, and earthquakes do not occur because of free will, so God could prevent them without limiting our free will at all. That is why I used natural evils as my examples. The value of free will cannot compensate for the suffering and death of babies with intestinal blockage, since their birth defects have nothing to do with free will.

Free will does show something about the problem of evil. It is logically possible that every bit of evil in the world results from an act of free will, so there is no truly natural evil. Even lightning and birth defects could be caused by free choices of invisible spirits. This

[handwritten marginal note: This is kind of funny.]

possibility is supposed to show that any evil is logically consistent with an all-good and all-powerful God. I am not sure whether these propositions really are consistent, since an all-powerful God might be able to stop such invisible spirits without depriving them of free will (as in the case of the pedophile above). Luckily, I need not settle this issue. My argument is not about logical consistency. It is about *evidence*. We have no reason whatsoever to believe in invisible spirits that cause evils that appear to be natural. In the absence of any such reason, we have evidence that these evils are natural, at least after we look hard but find no connection to anyone's free will. This evidence then gives us adequate reason to believe that the value of free will cannot justify God in allowing these evils.

The Standard Response: God's goodness is different from human goodness. He is good by His own standards, even though He allows evil with no compensating good.

Criticism: This response admits that God is not good by our common moral standards. This is hardly welcome news for anyone who wants a model to guide his life. It is hardly a God worth worshipping, except out of fear. It is not a God we could love or admire. We don't have any idea what to expect from such a God. In the future, will He allow or cause even more evil without compensation? Will this show that He is even better than before? Nobody can tell, if we cannot understand the standards by which God is deemed good.

Moreover, this response could justify atrocities. Imagine a human tyrant who kills and rapes or, at least, lets babies die painfully when he could save them easily. His followers claim that he is still a good person, because he has a divine right to rule without being subject to common moral standards. Whatever they say, however, we have plenty of reason to believe that this tyrant is not a good person. We should oppose him. God is no better if He lets babies die painfully for no adequate reason.

Some religious believers counter that, unlike a tyrant, God is not subject to our moral standards because He created us, so we owe Him everything. But that does not give God the right to abuse or neglect us any more than it gives human parents the right to abuse and neglect their children. Others say that our moral standards do not apply to God because He is so powerful. But a tyrant who is so powerful that nobody can stop him can still be judged to be morally bad. Might does not make right. This leaves no good reason to exempt God from moral judgment by our own standards.

The Modest Response: God has adequate reason to allow each bit of evil, but we cannot always see His reason, for we are just measly little humans.

Criticism: Anyone can try to defend any action, no matter how horrible, by saying that it is justified by some reason that we do not see. Suppose your neighbor lets his child suffer and starve. He has plenty of food and money, and his child seems normal, so you do not see anything to justify his neglect. Then his friend says, "Maybe he is a good person, and he has an adequate reason, but we just don't see it. Maybe this child's death will turn out for the best." You wouldn't buy this for a minute. You might give your neighbor a chance to defend his actions. However, if he *gives* no adequate reason when he could and would give one if he had one, then you would be justified in concluding that he *has* no adequate reason. Your conclusion would become even more secure if your neighbor let several of his children die in various horrible ways for no apparent reason. Similarly, if we look long and hard at a natural evil, such as an intestinal blockage, and we find nothing to suggest any adequate compensation, then we are justified in believing that there is no adequate compensation for that evil. This conclusion becomes more secure when the same pattern gets repeated in case after case after case.

We cannot be sure. It is always possible that some adequate compensation will arise centuries later by some obscure causal process of which we are now ignorant. However, we should not let uncertainty stop us from judging and acting when we have strong evidence. It is possible that our neighbor has his reasons for letting his children starve and that the children's deaths will work out for the best in the end, but we still may and should criticize and stop him. If we were not allowed to reach any conclusion without being completely sure, then we would never be allowed to reach any conclusion on any important matter, since we can never be completely sure about anything important (at least if it is controversial). The demand for certainty leads to ignorance and inaction.

Admittedly, we often lack strong evidence. Before we ask our neighbor what is going on, we might not have enough evidence to reach any conclusion, since most people know their own children and their own situation better than their nosy neighbors do. That is why we need to investigate carefully before we judge. However, after thorough investigation to the best of our abilities, if our neighbor reveals nothing and we see nothing that comes close to an adequate reason or suggests any promising avenue for further investigation, then we are justified in concluding that our neighbor has no adequate reason to let his children suffer and die. Analogously, if we look long and hard at a particular case of evil, but God reveals nothing and we see nothing that could compensate for that evil, and nothing that tells us where to look further, then it is reasonable to conclude that there actually will be no adequate compensation for this evil. Our justification becomes even stronger as we accumulate more and more evidence from more and more cases of natural evil.

This conclusion might seem rash if we would not be able to foresee an adequate compensation even if there were one. But why think that? The idea might be that compensation could come far in the future. That is possible, but we have no more reason to believe that the evil now will lead to great bliss in the long term than that this evil will lead to great misery. These speculations cancel each other, if there is any force to cancel in the first place. The idea might be that heaven awaits the suffering child, but I already criticized that response on the grounds that God could send the child straight to heaven without suffering. Add my criticisms of other responses, and then there is no plausible story about any adequate compensation for which we would not have evidence even if it were forthcoming.

Besides, why wouldn't God give us more evidence than we have on this matter? Why would He hide His light under a bushel? If He exists, He could easily show us His reasons for allowing evil. Our ignorance about His reasons is another form of evil, since it is a disability and causes distress to many people. So God would give us better evidence of adequate compensation for evil, if there were any.

It is still possible that God has a hidden reason. You might assume this if you already believe in God, but that assumption begs the question here. Just try to look at all of the evils in the world as you would if you were not already committed for or against the existence of God. Any neutral survey of the evidence is then bound to point away from the existence of God.

The Overriding Response: If there is a God, there must always be an adequate reason for evil, even if we cannot see it. Therefore, every argument for the existence of God is an argument that all evil is somehow compensated.

Criticism: Suppose you see your neighbor beat his child, then I claim that you must be hallucinating, since I have arguments to show that your neighbor is a good person who wouldn't beat his child. That would not convince you for a second unless my arguments were very strong. Similarly, the overriding response works only if there are very strong arguments for the existence of a traditional God. But there are none. This claim was supported by my criticisms of Craig's arguments in the first part of this book. It is also recognized by many Christians who espouse justification by faith rather than by reason or by acts.

Notice how much an argument would need to show to refute my argument from evil. It would not be enough to prove that the universe was created by a very powerful being. A refutation of my argument would have to show the existence of a God who is both all-good and all-powerful, since a limited creator is compatible with my argument. None of Craig's arguments comes close to showing that anything is both all-powerful and all-good. So none of Craig's arguments for the existence of God could undermine my argument against the existence of God.

Other arguments might be constructed, so I cannot be sure that no future argument will ever support the overriding response. All I (or anyone) can do is inspect each new argument when it is presented. Still, it is hard to imagine that any new argument for the existence of God will come close to proving the existence of an all-good and all-powerful God. Any argument that has eluded so many smart people for so long will not be very obvious, so it probably won't provide anything like the overwhelming amount of evidence that we have for the existence of so much natural evil with no compensating good. If no new argument is stronger than the evidence of evil, then no new argument for the existence of God can undermine my argument from evil against the existence of God.

Conclusion: Theists have a choice. They can say that God is not all-powerful, or they can say that God is not all-good. What they cannot do is face the evidence of evil in this world and still believe in the traditional Christian God who is both all-powerful and all-good. That is the only kind of God that we are arguing about here. So my argument shows that there is no God of the disputed kind.

2. The Problem of Action

In addition to being all-good and all-powerful, the traditional Christian God is also defined as eternal and active in time. These additional properties lead to new problems.

To say that God is eternal is to say that He exists outside of time. This kind of existence is mysterious, but it can be explained by analogy with numbers. The number three is what the numeral "3" refers to. A numeral is a symbol that can be written down at a particular time and place. In contrast, a number is not the kind of thing that can ever be written down.

To see how peculiar numbers are, consider how you would react if anyone said that the number three exists in North America but not in Antarctica. Antarctica lacks many things that we take for granted in North America, but not numbers. You know this without looking around Antarctica. What would you look for? This point about space applies also to time. If anyone said that, although the number three exists today, it did not exist in the days of dinosaurs, then you would sneer without checking the fossil record. Again, what would you check for? This shows that, if numbers exist, they do not exist at some times and places as opposed to others. Moreover, numbers exist or fail to exist equally at all times and places. A number cannot get bigger or smaller or change in any way.

These points about numbers are not controversial, but they are important here in two ways. First, atheists are sometimes accused of denying the existence of anything beyond the purely physical world. Some atheists do go that far, but other atheists admit the existence of non-physical minds and even abstract objects, including numbers. All that atheists have to deny is the existence of one kind of non-physical object, God. The more important lesson is that, if numbers exist outside of time, then they are eternal in the same way as God. This makes it fair to use numbers to determine what follows from the doctrine that God is eternal.

If the number three exists outside of time, this keeps it from causing any changes inside time. If you have triplets, that might make you very busy, but the number three itself cannot be what makes you busy. Why not? Because the number three is exactly the same when you are busy as when you are not. The number three was no different before, after, or as your triplets were born, so the number itself cannot explain why you became busy at the time when they were born.

More generally, the cause of any event must bear the right relation in time to that event. In a baseball game, if I swing at a pitch too soon, I will miss. If I swing too late, I will miss. The only way to hit a ball is to swing at just the right time (and in just the right place). If the number three exists outside of time, it cannot hit a ball or cause any event within time. Slogan: If you are not in time, you are inert.

The same restriction applies for the same reasons to any God who is outside of time. Such a God cannot change or exert force at just the right time, so He cannot cause changes within time. This result has been overlooked by many traditional Christian theologians, but it does follow from their doctrine of eternity.

The problem is that the traditional Christian God is also supposed to be active in time. He is supposed to have created the world, to cause miracles, to answer prayers, to be incarnated, and so on. None of this makes sense if God really is eternal and, hence, outside of time. If God has one of these traditional features, then He cannot have the other. Consequently, there cannot be a God who is both eternal and also active in time.

Theists sometimes respond by giving up the traditional doctrine that God exists outside of time. They claim instead that God is present equally, wholly, and indivisibly in each moment of time. This omnitemporal kind of God is not my target here, but it is worth showing why this move does not help anyway. If God makes the Red Sea part at noon, and if God is equally, wholly, and indivisibly present at midnight, then God would also have caused the Red Sea to part at midnight. Otherwise, His presence could not be sufficient to

cause the Red Sea to part at noon. More generally, nothing that exists equally, wholly, and indivisibly at all times can explain why an
event occurs at one time as opposed to earlier or later. That is why
God still cannot cause changes in time if He is equally, wholly, and
indivisibly present at each moment of time.

Another possible response is that laws of nature can be causes.
The law of gravity, for example, exists either outside time or at all
times. Yet this law might seem to cause balls to fall. This is inaccurate. A ball falls at a particular time and place because the earth at-
tracts it at that particular time and place. The ball would not move
in the same way if the earth were not there then, even though the
law of gravity would still hold without the earth. Thus, it is not the
law of gravity that causes the ball to fall. It is, instead, a particular
gravitational attraction in particular circumstances that causes the
ball to fall when, where, and how it does. Diffuse gravitational fields
and waves cause other effects, but all of these causes exist in time
and have properties that vary from one place to another, unlike God.

Gravity in general still might seem to be a causal factor instead of
a cause. Just as a match will not light without (some) oxygen, so the
ball will not fall without (some) gravity. Such background conditions
might seem analogous to an eternal or omnitemporal God, if events
in this world would not occur without God. This move, however, takes
us far away from any traditional notion of God. Neither gravity in
general nor the law of gravity can create worlds, cause miracles, answer prayers, make choices, lay down laws, or send sons to save us.
It would make no sense to worship gravity or the law of gravity. So
this analogy cannot salvage anything like the traditional notion of God.

In a final analogy, some theists say that God exists in a dimension
outside of time and space, but He can still have effects inside time
and space just as a three-dimensional pencil can cause marks on two-
dimensional paper. (Of course, paper has more than two dimensions,
but let's play along.) Still, the pencil must touch the paper at one
point but not another to make a mark at that one point but not the
other, so the pencil must be in some parts but not others of the paper's two dimensions, even if it exists in a third dimension as well.
Similarly, even if God did exist in some dimension other than time
and space, He would also have to exist in some parts of time and
space but not others (or He would have to exist in different ways in

different locations) in order to cause some effects but not others in our world of time and space. Such non-homogeneous existence is incompatible with the traditional notion of God.

Many more responses are possible here, as with the problem of evil. Theists might try to develop a new notion of causation that does not depend on temporal relations. This new kind of causation could take various forms, but each form is problematic, and I don't have time or space to go through them now. Instead, let's see how Craig responds. Then I will assess his response.

If no response is adequate, as I think, then theists have a choice, as with the problem of evil. They can claim that God is eternal but never active in time. Or they can claim that God is active in time but not eternal. What they cannot do is hold onto both parts of the traditional conception of God. The argument from action shows that there is no God of that traditional kind.

3. The Argument from Ignorance

My next argument cannot be escaped simply by giving up traditional features of God, since it applies to many other kinds of god. I will continue to focus on the traditional God, but any kind of god that cannot be supported by evidence runs afoul of a common standard for justified belief.

One principle that is accepted throughout science and everyday life is that we should not believe in entities for which we have no evidence. No good scientist would believe in a new element or particle or force without evidence. Any scientist who did claim to have discovered a new particle but who could not produce any evidence for it would be laughed out of town.

This rule applies with special force when an entity is unusual in important respects. If someone believes that there are clothes in my closet, then he might not seem to need any evidence for this belief other than his past experiences of closets, most of which contained clothes. However, no evidence like this is available, and the need for evidence seems especially strong, when someone believes in a kind of entity that is unprecedented. Nobody should believe that there is a perfect shirt or an invisibility cloak in the closet without any evidence for the existence of such an oddity. I hope everyone agrees in that case.

Religion might seem different. Religion is often said to be immune from the standards of science, because it lies outside the realm where evidence is possible. But this view leads to absurdity. If the fact that a religious belief cannot be subject to evidence did license one to accept that belief without evidence, then the same principle would also license many ridiculous beliefs.

An amusing example occurs in Charles Schultz's cartoon, *Peanuts*. Linus believes in the Great Pumpkin, who visits pumpkin patches all over the world every Halloween. Linus has no evidence *for* his belief, since he has never seen the Great Pumpkin, and Linus can explain all of his beliefs and experiences without postulating any Great Pumpkin. On the other hand, Linus also ensures that nobody can have any evidence *against* the Great Pumpkin, since it is visible only to those with a pure heart. Linus stays in a pumpkin patch all Halloween night (at a great cost in candy). He looks constantly and carefully for the Great Pumpkin (at a great cost in sleep). But he sees nothing. Still, this does not show that the Great Pumpkin does not exist. All it shows is that Linus's heart was not pure, or not pure enough, at least according to Linus. This doctrine thus makes it impossible to prove that Linus is wrong. Moreover, Linus might be right. It is possible (just barely!) that there is a Great Pumpkin. However, most people agree that Linus is not justified in believing in the Great Pumpkin. More strongly, Linus *should not* believe in the Great Pumpkin. That is what makes the cartoon so funny. Linus is the butt of jokes in a cartoon for kids, because Linus believes something that he should not believe, given his evidence, on standards that are obvious even to children.

Linus illustrates why we should not believe in unusual entities without evidence for their existence and why this common restriction cannot be avoided by formulating one's beliefs to make them incapable of refutation. If we weaken our epistemic standards to accommodate irrefutable beliefs, then we might end up believing in the Great Pumpkin or, at least, holding that many absurd beliefs like this are justified.

The same standards apply to beliefs about God. If there is no evidence for God's existence, then we ought not to believe that God exists. This follows even if God were defined so as to remove any possibility of evidence against His existence.

But is there evidence for God? Craig claims that there is. That is why he gave several arguments for the existence of God in the first part of this book. However, I refuted every one of his arguments. Craig might have overlooked an even better argument. Or maybe there is some way to get around my criticisms. But I don't see any.

Religious experiences are sometimes seen as evidence for God. Many people have feelings that seem to them to come from a higher power outside of them. But many people also think that they see and hear ghosts. Their experiences are not evidence for ghosts because we and they have no independent reason to think that their experiences are accurate rather than illusions. By the same standards, when people seem to experience God, that is no evidence for God because they and we have no independent reason to believe that their religious experiences are accurate rather than illusions. Moreover, we and they have plenty of reason to suspect that there is some better explanation of why they seem to see God. Just as people see ghosts only when they are afraid and predisposed to believe in ghosts, so people experience God only when they are predisposed to believe in God and are gripped by emotions that often distort experiences. God might appear only to those who seek or believe in Him, but then those experiences cannot count as evidence for God. Finally, even if religious experiences were evidence for something, they could not be evidence that their source is all-good and all-powerful. The most vivid religious experience could result from a God who is very powerful and pretty good, so they cannot be evidence for a traditional God.

Miracles are also often claimed to be evidence for God. However, second-hand reports of miracles are dubious at best, for obvious reasons (which I cited in the first part of this book). On the other hand, if you think that you have witnessed a miracle first-hand, then the circumstances need to be considered carefully. Even if you and I cannot come up with any natural explanation for what you observed, that is no more miraculous than most magic tricks are. Besides, no miracle can be evidence that God is all-powerful or all-good, which is the kind of God at issue here.

I conclude that neither arguments nor experiences nor miracles provide any good evidence for the existence of God. This conclusion, together with common standards for justified belief, implies that we ought not to believe that God exists and, hence, that we ought to believe that God does not exist.

Theists often respond that it is fallacious to argue from "We have no evidence for it" to "It does not exist." This is called an argument from ignorance. Many logic textbooks label it a fallacy.

I admit that many arguments of this form are fallacious. One cannot say that there is no gold on Uranus just because we do not have any evidence for gold on Uranus. The problem is clear: Even if there were gold on Uranus, we still would not (or, at least, might not) have evidence for it. That is why we cannot conclude that there is no gold on Uranus.

However, this point cannot be used to defend the claim that there is gold on Uranus. If there is no evidence for gold on Uranus, maybe we should not conclude that there is none, but we also should not believe that there is some. We should suspend belief until we have adequate evidence one way or the other. Consequently, this analogy cannot provide solace to religious believers. If belief in God is like belief in gold on Uranus, then the lack of evidence for God does not show that God does not exist. However, the lack of evidence also cannot be used to defend a belief in God, since it supports agnostics who hold that we should suspend belief until we have evidence (even if this is a very long time).

More importantly, arguments from ignorance are not *always* fallacious. Arguments of this form work fine when the phenomenon is something that we would know if it were true. If I had a pot-bellied pig on my head, I would know it, at least after I felt around up there. Thus, my lack of evidence for a pot-bellied pig on my head is adequate reason for me to believe that there is none. Not everything is as obvious as a pot-bellied pig. But doctors can also have adequate reason to believe that a patient does not have a virus, if they look closely, they find no evidence for that virus, and the patient would have easily detectable symptoms if the patient did have that virus.

That is the situation with God. If there were an all-good and all-powerful God who could act in time, then we would have better evidence than we have. He could easily reveal himself by appearing before us. Giving us better evidence would not harm us. Why would such a God hide? Does he hide?

Some theists answer that, if the evidence for God were stronger, believers would not need faith. However, better evidence could leave room for faith. I have faith in my wife's love, even though I also have strong evidence of her love, namely, that she puts up with me! I would not be better off if I had to rely more on faith because I had less evidence for her love. So why is it better to have less evidence for God?

One answer might be that better evidence would take away our freedom not to believe. However, evidence does not take away any valuable kind of freedom. If it did, teachers would restrict the freedom of their students every time the teachers told the students a fact about history or performed a science experiment. If any freedom is lost in such revelations, it is a kind of freedom that is not very valuable, since it is just the freedom to believe irrationally.

Finally, even if stronger evidence did have some costs, it would also have many benefits. The new evidence would remove or reduce nagging doubts, as well as any fears that your children or friends might disavow God and end up in Hell. It would bring assurance and solace, if God is as merciful as Christians claim. Most evil people would be scared away from their horrible deeds, since few, if any, people would rape and torture if they received strong evidence that such deeds would be punished with eternal torment.

With so little to lose and so much to gain, an all-good God would reveal Himself clearly to everyone. An all-powerful God could easily reveal Himself clearly to everyone. But God has not revealed Himself clearly to everyone. Even if you have been convinced by your religious experiences, there are billions of other people on this earth now and in the past who have little or no evidence of God. Just ask yourself honestly, "Could God reveal Himself more clearly?" The answer is bound to be "Yes," since God is supposed to be all-powerful. Now ask yourself honestly, "What reason does God have not to reveal Himself more clearly?" I doubt that you can come up with any reason that withstands honest and thorough reflection. Consequently, if there were a God, we would have more and better evidence than we do. That is why our lack of evidence for God supports my thesis that there is no God.

4. Conclusion

Taken together, my arguments lead to the conclusion that no traditional God exists. As I said, my arguments do not pretend to be conclusive proofs, but they do provide strong evidence against any traditional God.

Even if theists accept my arguments, they can still believe in other kinds of God. Religious rituals and institutions can continue. They can still follow the central moral teachings of the great religions. My arguments show why theists should believe that no traditional God exists, but their everyday lives can still go on much as they did before. To that extent, theists have nothing important to fear from my conclusion.

Indeed, there is much to gain from my conclusion. The joys of inquiry unfettered by dogma are intense. The resulting knowledge is valuable in itself, as is the removal of any kind of ignorance and illusion. The knowledge that God does not exist also has good consequences. If people stop looking to Heaven for solutions to their problems, then they should work harder to solve the many problems in this world.

Even if this picture is overly optimistic, and life is better when people believe in a traditional God, that good life would then depend on an illusion, since that God does not exist. My main concern is not to make people comfortable but to determine whether the traditional God really does exist. He does not.

CHAPTER 5

Theism Undefeated

William Lane Craig

The outspoken Madelyn Murray O'Hare once remarked, "Agnostics are just atheists without guts." Professor Sinnott-Armstrong has guts. He is not content to rest in an easy and undemanding agnosticism; rather he argues that we have "strong evidence," if not conclusive proof, that God does *not* exist. He presents three arguments in support of his claim: the problem of evil, the problem of action, and the problem of ignorance. Since the first of these three problems is by far the most compelling (at least emotionally), whereas the latter two can be fairly easily answered, I'll consider them in reverse order.

The Argument from Ignorance

This argument is based on the principle that "we should not believe in entities for which we have no evidence." Since we have no evidence for God, we should not believe in Him.

The shortcoming of this argument is that even if we accept its underlying principle (which is not uncontroversial[1]), it at best supports agnosticism, not atheism. Therefore, it cannot count among Sinnott-Armstrong's "positive arguments for atheism."

The careful reader will note a subtle but crucial shift as the argument unfolds. Initially Sinnott-Armstrong asserts, "If there is no evidence for God's existence, then we ought not to believe that God exists." This is a careful application of his principle and enunciates an agnostic position. But a page later, he asserts, "This [the absence of good evidence for God], together with common standards for justified belief, implies that we ought not to believe that God exists and, hence, that we ought to believe that God does not exist." Did you notice the shift from "we ought not to believe that God exists" to "we ought to believe that God does not exist"? That shift, which represents the move from agnosticism to atheism, requires justification. To borrow Sinnott-Armstrong's example, in the absence of evidence, we should not believe that there is gold on Uranus; but it does not follow that we should believe that there is no gold on Uranus. Thus, even if entirely successful, the argument so far does nothing to support atheism.

In a bizarre role reversal, Sinnott-Armstrong rejoins, "However, this point cannot be used to defend the claim that there is gold on Uranus. If there is no evidence for gold on Uranus, maybe we should not conclude that there is none, but we also should not believe that there is some." Wait a minute! I thought this was supposed to be a positive argument for atheism. But at best this implies that we should neither believe that God exists nor believe that He does not exist. That is classic agnosticism, not atheism. Worse, Sinnott-Armstrong goes on to say, "the lack of evidence also cannot be used to defend a belief in God." But I don't know of anyone who thinks that the existence of God follows from the *lack* of evidence (indeed, isn't such a claim incoherent when you think about it?). Sinnott-Armstrong has shifted from building a positive case for atheism to knocking down straw men.

Cognizant of the weakness of his argument, Sinnott-Armstrong proceeds to argue that in certain cases the absence of evidence for some thing is evidence of the absence of that thing. If we should expect to see evidence of some thing if it did exist, then the absence of any such evidence gives us grounds to think it does not exist. That seems quite right. The absence of evidence for an elephant in this room constitutes good grounds for thinking there is no elephant in this room, for if there were an elephant here, I should expect to see evidence of it. By contrast, the absence of evidence for a flea in this room provides no grounds at all for my thinking that there is no flea in this room, since if there were a flea here, I shouldn't expect things to look any different than they do.

So the whole question devolves to Sinnott-Armstrong's claim that "If there were an all-good and all-powerful God, then we would have better evidence than we have." I have to say honestly that I just have no confidence at all that this is true. Indeed, this claim strikes me as enormously presumptuous.[2] Who are we to say what kind of evidence God would give of His existence if He existed?

The question is not, as Sinnott-Armstrong thinks, "Could God reveal Himself more clearly?" Of course, He could: He could have inscribed the label "Made by God" on every atom or planted a neon cross in the heavens with the message "Jesus Saves." But why should He want to do such a thing? Although I've found that atheists have a hard time grasping this, it is a fact that in the Christian view it is a matter of relative indifference to God whether people (merely) believe that He exists or not. For what God is interested in is building a love relationship with you, not just getting you to believe that He exists. According to the Bible, even the demons believe that God exists—and tremble, for they have no saving relationship with Him (James 2.19). Of course, in order to believe *in* God, you must believe *that* God exists. But there is no reason at all to think that if God were to make His existence more manifest, more people would come into a saving relationship with Him. Mere showmanship will not bring about a change of heart (Luke 16.30–31). It's interesting that, as the Bible describes the history of God's dealings with mankind, there has been a progressive "interiorization" of this interaction. In the Old Testament, God is described as revealing Himself to His people in manifest wonders: the plagues upon Egypt, the pillar of fire and smoke, the parting of the Red Sea. But did such wonders produce lasting heart-change in the people? No, Israel fell into apostasy with tiresome repetitiveness. If God were to inscribe His name on every atom or place a neon cross in the sky, people might believe that He exists, all right, but what confidence could we have that after a time they would not begin to chafe under the brazen advertisements of their Creator and even to resent such effrontery? According to the New Testament, not only is God's existence revealed through His handiwork in nature, so that unbelievers are "without excuse" (Romans 1.20), and His moral law written on the hearts of all persons (Romans 2.14–15), rendering them morally culpable before God, but His Holy Spirit ministers to the heart of every person convicting and drawing him to God (John 16.7–11). Moreover, God in His omniscience has providentially ordered the world so that people are born at times and places conducive to their coming to faith (Acts 17.24–27). Do we have any reason to think that if God's existence were more manifest in the way that Sinnott-Armstrong envisions, this would be any more effective in drawing people into a saving relationship with God than the interior way that He has chosen? I think an unprejudiced answer to this question can only be that this is pure speculation on Sinnott-Armstrong's part. He has no idea at all that in a world of free creatures in which God's existence is as obvious as the nose on your face that more people would come to love Him and know His salvation than in the actual world. But then the claim that if God existed, He would make His existence more evident has little or no warrant, thereby undermining the further claim that the absence of such evidence is itself positive evidence that God does not exist. The whole argument is a tissue of uncertainties.

The Problem of Action

Sinnott-Armstrong argues that if God is timeless, then He cannot be causally active in the temporal world, as the Christian faith holds Him to be. Therefore, traditional theism is internally inconsistent and cannot be true.

I have to confess that I was rather pleased to find this objection in Sinnott-Armstrong's repertoire, since it constitutes an endorsement of precisely the position that I have labored to establish in my own work on the nature of divine eternity. The Bible affirms that God is eternal in the sense that He is without beginning or end. He never came into nor will He ever go out of existence. But the Bible leaves it open as to whether we are to understand divine eternity as timelessness (atemporality) or as everlasting duration (omnitemporality). Typically, the Bible speaks of God's being eternal in the sense of being omnitemporal, that is, enduring through every time that there is (Psalm 90.2). Indeed, Padgett in his study of divine eternity flatly concludes, "the Bible knows nothing of a timeless divine eternity in the traditional sense."[3] I think Padgett's exegesis fails to reckon sufficiently with biblical texts that seem to contemplate time's having had a beginning (Genesis 1.1; Proverbs 8.22–23; Jude 25; Titus 1.2–3; II Timothy 1.9). But the point remains that the Bible does not teach that God is timeless. The nature of divine eternity is a question to be answered by philosophical, not biblical, theology.

I have elsewhere argued that in being related to a temporal world, God, even if intrinsically changeless, nonetheless undergoes extrinsic change; that is to say, He changes in His relations with temporal things, and therefore cannot be timeless.[4] Therefore, so long as a temporal world exists, God must exist in time. On my view, God is timeless without creation and temporal with creation.

Thus, ironically, this second "objection," far from proving atheism, is actually one that I have defended even more vigorously than Sinnott-Armstrong. He does object that "nothing that exists equally, wholly, and indivisibly at all times can explain why an event occurs at one time as opposed to earlier or later." At first we might think this assertion patently false. I, for example, exist equally, wholly, and indivisibly at every moment of my existence, and I obviously cause certain events to occur when they do rather than earlier or later. But the reason Sinnott-Armstrong makes his claim is because he is a determinist.[5] Although he says he believes in free will, his understanding of freedom is a compatibilist, not a libertarian, understanding. On such a view, we are "free," even though our decisions and actions are determined by antecedent causes, if those decisions and actions are voluntary, or in line with what we want. On a deterministic view, once all the causal factors sufficient for an effect exist, then the effect must exist, too. So if the cause of some event is equally, wholly, and indivisibly present at a time t_0, then the effect cannot be delayed in its appearance until some later time t_n; rather it must exist at t_0. That's why Sinnott-Armstrong says that if God is the cause of the Red Sea's parting, then if God exists at midnight, the Red Sea must part at midnight.

The discerning reader will notice that this is basically the same reasoning I employed in defense of the personhood of the transcendent cause of the universe established by the cosmological argument.[6] The origin of the universe cannot be explained as the effect of a deterministic cause, for if the cause were eternally present (in either a temporal or an atemporal sense), then the effect would be equally present as well. The only way to get an effect that begins in time from an eternal cause is by adopting a wholly different, indeterministic account of causation: agent causation.[7] An agent endowed with libertarian free will can bring about new effects in time without deterministic, antecedent conditions. That is why agents (like ourselves or God) can exist equally, wholly, and indivisibly at various times and yet effect new and different events at various times. It need only be added that Sinnott-Armstrong has said nothing to show that libertarian freedom or agent causation does not exist. So once again, the reasoning endorsed by Sinnott-Armstrong only goes to support the theistic position.

The Problem of Evil

Now we come to a really serious problem, atheism's killer argument, the problem of evil. Since Sinnott-Armstrong makes it clear that he is not defining evil to have a moral dimension but means merely anything harmful, it will be less misleading if we characterize his argument as the problem of harm or suffering.

The problem of suffering is undoubtedly the greatest obstacle to belief in God—both for the Christian and the non-Christian. When I consider the depth and extent of suffering in the world, then I have to admit that it makes it hard to believe in God. No one who is not deranged can contemplate the many examples of innocent suffering listed by Sinnott-Armstrong and not be deeply moved and troubled by them. Their emotional impact is undeniable and makes it difficult to believe that an all-powerful and all-good God exists.

But as Sinnott-Armstrong recognizes, we as philosophers are called upon, not just to express how we feel about some issue, but to reflect rigorously and dispassionately about it. And despite the undeniable *emotional* impact of the problem of suffering, I am persuaded that as a strictly rational, intellectual problem, the problem of suffering does not constitute a disproof of the existence of God. It will therefore be helpful if we distinguish between the *intellectual* problem of suffering and the *emotional* problem of suffering. The intellectual problem concerns how to give a rational account of the co-existence of God and suffering. The emotional problem concerns how to dissolve the emotional dislike people have of a God who would permit such suffering. The intellectual problem lies in the province of the philosopher; the emotional problem lies in the province of the counselor. It's important to keep this distinction clear because the solution to the intellectual problem is apt to appear dry and uncomforting to someone who is going through suffering, whereas the solution to the emotional problem is apt to appear superficial and explanatorily deficient to someone contemplating the question abstractly.

Now, philosophers usually distinguish two ways in which the intellectual problem of suffering may be cast, the *logical version* or the *evidential version*. I think the traditional distinction can be more clearly and accurately made, however, if we make a distinction between the problem of suffering as an *internal* problem or as an *external* problem for Christian theism. That is to say, the problem may be presented in terms of premises to which the Christian theist is committed as a Christian, so that the Christian world view is allegedly somehow at odds with itself. On the other hand, the problem may be presented in terms of premises to which the Christian theist is not committed as a Christian but which we nonetheless have good reason to regard as true. The first approach tries to expose an inner tension within the Christian world view itself; the second approach attempts to present evidence against the truth of the Christian world view.

It's worth emphasizing that traditionally, atheists have claimed that the problem of suffering constitutes an internal problem for Christian theism. That is, atheists have claimed that the statements

A. An all-powerful, all-good God exists.

and

B. Suffering exists (in various kinds and quantities).

are either logically inconsistent or improbable with respect to each other. As a result of the work of Christian philosophers like Alvin Plantinga, it is today widely recognized that the internal problem of suffering is a failure as an argument for atheism. No one has ever been able to show that (A) and (B) are either logically incompatible with each other or improbable with respect to each other. For there is no way to prove, given the existence of God, that it is impossible or improbable that God has some morally sufficient reason for permitting any observed instance of suffering. This is a tremendous encouragement as we deal with remaining questions on which no consensus yet exists (and constitutes as well a decisive refutation of the attitude that philosophy never makes any progress!).

Having abandoned the internal problem of suffering, atheists have very recently taken to advocating the external problem, often called the evidential problem of evil. Sinnott-Armstrong's argument represents a statement of this external problem. His four-point argument can be simplified if we take God to be essentially all-powerful and all-good and call suffering that is not necessary to achieve some adequately compensating good "gratuitous suffering." His argument can be summarized in three steps:

1. If God exists, gratuitous suffering does not exist.
2. Gratuitous suffering exists.
3. Therefore, God does not exist.

Sinnott-Armstrong's argument is not that suffering itself disproves God. Rather he's talking about a very special *kind* of suffering, namely uncompensated, unnecessary suffering. It is *this* kind of suffering that is said to be incompatible with God's existence. Sinnott-Armstrong maintains that this special kind of suffering exists, and therefore God does not exist. What makes this an external problem is that the Christian is not committed by his world view to the truth of (2). The Christian is committed to the truth that *suffering exists*, but not that *gratuitous suffering exists*. Thus the atheist claims that the apparently uncompensated and unnecessary suffering in the world constitutes *evidence* against God's existence.

Now, the most controversial premise in this argument is step (2). Everybody admits that the world is filled with *apparently* gratuitous suffering. We are often unable to see any reason for why harm befalls us. But that doesn't imply that these apparently gratuitous evils really *are* gratuitous. Every one of us can think back on experiences of suffering or hardship in our lives, which at the time seemed pointless and unnecessary but, when viewed in retrospect, are seen to have been ultimately to our or others' advantage, even if we would not want to go through them again. The key move in the atheist's argument, then, will be his inference from apparently gratuitous suffering to genuinely gratuitous suffering.

In examining this key inference, we should do well to note two general weaknesses in Sinnott-Armstrong's style of argument. First, he typically reasons by analogy, comparing God's relation to us with our relation to our neighbor. The problem with this method of argument in general is that any disanalogy in the comparison undermines the force of the argument. And in this case in particular God's relationship to us is strikingly disanalogous to our relationships to our neighbors. For we and our neighbors are peers; but God is our Creator and Sovereign. Thus, I am not charged with the moral education of my neighbor; but God aims that we should learn to become mature moral agents. I am not responsible for the eternal salvation of my neighbor; but God is involved in drawing not only my neighbor but all people to a saving knowledge of Himself. I am bound by certain moral obligations and prohibitions vis à vis my neighbor (e.g., not to take his life); but God (if He has moral duties at all) is not bound by many of these (e.g., He can give and take life as He pleases). These and other disanalogies considerably weaken Sinnott-Armstrong's argument from analogy.

The tenuousness of such analogical reasoning is particularly egregious in his criticism of what he calls the "Glorious Response." A human father who thought of himself as the end-all of his children's existence would indeed be egomaniacal. But the infinite God, who is the locus of goodness and love, is the appropriate end of all beings (even of Himself!), the *summum bonum* (highest good). Of course, God cares whether we are happy, and He knows that true happiness and human fulfillment are found in our knowing the highest good. Therefore, His loving purpose for humankind is to draw people freely into a saving relationship with Himself. The real question is, as Sinnott-Armstrong asserts, whether "God can surely find some more effective and efficient way to lead people to glorify Him." I think we have no inkling whatsoever that this is the case: it is sheer speculation. Be that as it may, the analogy of the human father is so deeply flawed as to be worthless.

Second, Sinnott-Armstrong's method of dealing with proffered solutions to the problem of suffering is the strategy of "divide and conquer." That is to say, he typically refutes a solution by arguing that it cannot cover *all* cases of suffering. What he fails to appreciate is that God's reasons for permitting suffering are doubtlessly complex and multifarious. That implies that no one solution is intended to cover all cases of suffering. So take, for example, what Sinnott-Armstrong calls the "Virtuous Response." Like it or not, it is an undeniable fact that moral development is impossible without hardship and suffering; without them we would be pampered and spoiled children, heedless of the consequences of our actions and indifferent toward others, rather than responsible and wise adults with a virtuous moral character. Sinnott-Armstrong responds in part by charging that such a solution is "unfair" to babies who suffer and die for the moral development of parents. But that charge falls to the ground when the Virtuous Response is conjoined with the so-called "Heavenly Response," for the child receives a compensation so incomprehensibly great that it is incommensurable with the suffering. Sinnott-Armstrong's complaint about the Heavenly Response is that God could send babies directly to heaven. But that forgets the Virtuous Response: so doing would short-circuit God's work in the lives of the parents or other people. What Sinnott-Armstrong's "divide and conquer" strategy fails to understand is that the solutions are complementary and mutually reinforcing.

Apart from these general problems of Sinnott-Armstrong's methodology, let me suggest three reasons why I think that the inference from apparently gratuitous suffering to genuinely gratuitous suffering is tenuous.

1. *We are not in a good position to assess with confidence the probability that God lacks morally sufficient reasons for permitting the suffering in the world.* Whether the suffering in the world really is gratuitous depends on whether God has morally sufficient reasons for permitting the suffering that occurs. What makes the probability here so difficult to assess is that we are not in a good position to make these kinds of probability judgments with any sort of confidence. The philosopher William Alston has surveyed six cognitive limitations under which we labor which impair such judgments, including: lack of data, complexity greater than we can handle, difficulty in knowing what is metaphysically possible, ignorance of the range of possibilities, ignorance of the range of values, and limits of our capacity to make well-considered value judgments. He concludes, "The judgments required by the inductive argument from evil are of a very special and enormously ambitious type, and our cognitive capacities are not equal to this one. . . . it is in principle impossible for us to be justified in supposing that God does not have sufficient reasons for permitting evil that are unknown to us."[8]

Take just the first of these limits: our lack of data. As finite persons limited in space and time, we experience a brief glimpse of the history of the world. But in the Christian view, the transcendent and sovereign God sees the end of history from its beginning and providentially orders history so that His purposes are ultimately achieved through human free decisions. Only an omniscient mind could grasp the complexities of directing a world of free creatures toward one's pre-visioned goals. One has only to think of the innumerable, incalculable contingencies involved in arriving at a single historical event, say, the Allied victory at D-day. In order to bring about this event through the actions of free creatures, God might well have to put up with myriad evils along the way. We simply have no idea of the natural and moral evils that might be involved in order for God to arrange the circumstances and the free agents required to achieve such an intended purpose. Suffering that appears pointless or unnecessary to us within our limited framework may be seen to have been justly permitted from within God's wider framework.

To borrow an illustration from a developing field of science, Chaos theory, scientists have discovered that certain macroscopic systems—for example, weather systems or insect populations—are extraordinarily sensitive to the tiniest perturbations. A butterfly fluttering on a branch in West Africa may set in motion forces that would eventually result in a hurricane over the Atlantic Ocean. Yet it is impossible in principle for anyone observing that butterfly palpitating on a branch to predict such an outcome.[9] The brutal murder of an innocent man or a child's dying of leukemia could send a ripple effect through history so that God's morally sufficient reason for permitting it might not emerge until centuries later or perhaps in another country. Given our limited perspective, we cannot always discern what reasons a provident God might have in mind for permitting some harm to enter our lives. Certainly, much suffering seems pointless and unnecessary to us—but we are simply not in a position to say.

In this light, we see the shortcoming of Sinnott-Armstrong's reply to what he calls the "Modest Response." The problem with his appeal to human analogies is precisely that the neighbor shares the same cognitive limitations that we do, and therefore we can confidently judge that he lacks any morally sufficient reason for letting his child starve. Thus, Sinnott-Armstrong's conclusion that the Modest Response allows anyone to "defend any action, no matter how horrible, by saying that there is some reason that we do not see," does not follow. He admits that in the case of a provident God some adequate compensation might arise for an apparently gratuitous evil centuries later by a causal chain we do not discern; but he insists that "we should not let uncertainty stop us from judging and acting when we have strong evidence." But the question is, of course, whether we do or even can have such evidence in the case of God. What, exactly, would constitute "strong evidence" that God in His providence does not have a morally sufficient reason, which will emerge in the future for permitting some harm in the present? I doubt that Sinnott-Armstrong could provide any criteria for what constitutes such strong evidence.

His realization of the shortcoming of his argument becomes clear when he tries once more to shift the burden of proof: future compensation is possible, he admits, "but we have no more reason to believe that the evil now will lead to great bliss in the long term than that this evil will lead to great misery." Any positive argument for atheism is herewith quietly abandoned. My point is precisely that we are not in a position to make these sorts of probability judgments either way. We do not know the outcome of even seemingly trivial events, whether good or ill. Even contemporary filmmakers seem to appreciate this truth, as evidenced in the movie "Sliding Doors," in which a young woman's life takes two radically different courses depending upon the seemingly trivial event of whether she makes it through the sliding doors of a subway train she wants to catch. One course of her life leads to suffering and disaster, while the other leads to prosperity and success—all based upon whether a little girl playing with her dolly blocks the young woman's path for a split second as she hurries to the train! Most intriguingly, however, we discover in the movie's end that it is really the life of suffering and hardship that turns out to be the best life, while the seemingly happy life leads to her premature death. The film brilliantly illustrates the impossibility of our forming with any confidence probability judgments that some particular instance of suffering is in fact gratuitous and that God does not have a morally sufficient reason for permitting it.

To say this is not to appeal to mystery, but rather to point to the inherent cognitive limitations that frustrate attempts to say that it is improbable that God has a morally sufficient reason for permitting some particular harm. As Alston says, "We are simply not in a position to justifiably assert that God would have no sufficient reason for permitting evil."[10] Once we reflect on God's providence over the whole of history and on how seemingly insignificant events can derail the course of history with ever-widening consequences, then it becomes evident how hopeless it is for limited observers to speculate on the probability of God's lacking morally sufficient reasons for the suffering that we see. We are simply not in a good position to assess such probabilities with any confidence.

It's interesting that Sinnott-Armstrong's final attempt to deal with the Modest Response is to complain once more of the hiddenness of God: God, if He existed, would tell us what His morally sufficient reasons are for permitting suffering to overtake us. And once again I think we can repose no confidence at all in such a presumptuous assertion. Moreover, the demand is wholly unreasonable. First, since there is no one reason for God's permitting suffering, such a revelation would have to be imparted to every person on every occasion of suffering throughout the history of the world. That would turn the universe into a haunted house. Second, such a revelation might be self-negating in many cases. If God were to reveal to us why He permitted us to suffer some particular evil, then our having that knowledge might lead to the frustration of God's purpose. For example, the free agents might then act in ways other than they would have acted if they had lacked the knowledge, so that as a result, a future compensating event might not take place—in which case that could not have been the reason why God permitted the harm! Thus, the envisioned revelation might lead to self-stultifying situations. The demand is then logically impossible to meet.

2. *Christian theism entails doctrines that increase the probability that suffering would appear to be gratuitous, even though it's not.* This makes it all the harder for Sinnott-Armstrong to justifiably infer from the *appearance* of gratuitous evil to the *fact* of gratuitous evil. What are some of these doctrines? Let me mention three:

Doctrine #1: *The purpose of life is not human happiness as such, but knowing God.*

One reason that the suffering in the world seems pointless is that we tend naturally to assume that if God exists, then His purpose for human life is happiness in this world. God's role is to provide a comfortable environment for His human pets. But in the Christian view, this is false. We are not God's pets, and the goal of human life is not happiness as such, but the knowledge of God—which in the end will bring true and everlasting human fulfillment. Many evils occur in life that are utterly gratuitous with respect to the goal of producing human happiness; but they may not be gratuitous with respect to producing a deeper knowledge of God. Innocent human suffering provides an occasion for deeper dependency and trust in God, either on the part of the sufferer or those around him. Of course, as Sinnott-Armstrong reminds us, whether God's purpose is achieved through our suffering will depend on our response. Do we respond with anger and bitterness toward God, or do we turn to Him in faith for strength to endure? God may well be less concerned with what we go through than with our attitude while going through it.

Because God's ultimate goal for humanity is the knowledge of Himself—which alone can bring eternal happiness to creatures—history cannot be seen in its true perspective apart from the Kingdom of God. Martyn Lloyd-Jones has written,

The key to the history of the world is the kingdom of God. . . . From the very beginning, . . . God has been at work establishing a new kingdom in the world. It is His own kingdom, and He is calling people out of the world into that kingdom: and everything that happens in the world has relevance to it. . . . Other events are of importance as they have a bearing upon that event. The problems of today are to be understood only in its light. . . .

Let us not therefore be stumbled when we see surprising things happening in the world. Rather let us ask, 'What is the relevance of this event to the kingdom of God?' Or, if strange things are happening to you personally, don't complain but say, 'What is God teaching me through this?' . . . We need not become bewildered and doubt the love or the justice of God. . . . We should . . . judge every event in the light of God's great, eternal and glorious purpose.[11]

It may well be the case that natural and moral evils are part of the means God uses to draw people into His Kingdom. A reading of a missions handbook, such as Patrick Johnstone's *Operation World*, reveals that it is precisely in countries that have endured severe hardship that evangelical Christianity is growing at its greatest rate, while growth curves in the indulgent West are nearly flat. Consider, for example, the following reports:[12]

China: It is estimated that 20 million Chinese lost their lives during Mao's Cultural Revolution. Christians stood firm in what was probably the most widespread and harsh persecution the Church has ever experienced. The persecution purified and indigenized the Church. Since 1977, the growth of the Church in China has no parallels in history. Researchers estimated there were 30–75 million Christians by 1990. Mao Zedong unwittingly became the greatest evangelist in history.

El Salvador: The 12-year civil war, earthquakes, and the collapse of the price of coffee, the nation's main export, impoverished the nation. Over 80% live in dire poverty. An astonishing spiritual harvest has been gathered from all strata of society in the midst of the hate and bitterness of war. In 1960, evangelicals were 2.3% of the population, but today are around 20%.

Ethiopia: Ethiopia is in a state of shock. Her population struggles with the trauma of millions of deaths through repression, famine, and war. Two great waves of violent persecution refined and purified the Church, but there were many martyrs. There have been millions coming to Christ. Protestants were fewer than 0.8% of the population in 1960, but by 1990 this may have become 13% of the population.

Examples such as these could be multiplied. The history of mankind has been a history of suffering and war. Yet it has also been a history of the advance of the Kingdom of God. Figure 1 is a chart released in 1990 by the U.S. Center for World Mission documenting the growth in evangelical Christianity over the centuries.

According to Johnstone, "We are living in the time of the largest ingathering of people into the Kingdom of God that the world has ever seen."[13] It is not at all improbable that this astonishing growth

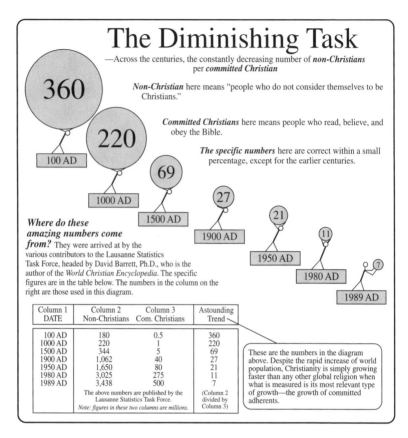

The Diminishing Task

—Across the centuries, the constantly decreasing number of *non-Christians* per *committed Christian*

360

100 AD

220

1000 AD

Non-Christian here means "people who do not consider themselves to be Christians."

Committed Christians here means people who read, believe, and obey the Bible.

The specific numbers here are correct within a small percentage, except for the earlier centuries.

69

1500 AD

27

1900 AD

21

1950 AD

11

1980 AD

7

1989 AD

Where do these amazing numbers come from? They were arrived at by the various contributors to the Lausanne Statistics Task Force, headed by David Barrett, Ph.D., who is the author of the *World Christian Encyclopedia*. The specific figures are in the table below. The numbers in the column on the right are those used in this diagram.

Column 1 DATE	Column 2 Non-Christians	Column 3 Com. Christians	Astounding Trend
100 AD	180	0.5	360
1000 AD	220	1	220
1500 AD	344	5	69
1900 AD	1,062	40	27
1950 AD	1,650	80	21
1980 AD	3,025	275	11
1989 AD	3,438	500	7
	The above numbers are published by the Lausanne Statistics Task Force.		(Column 2 divided by Column 3)
	Note: figures in these two columns are millions.		

These are the numbers in the diagram above. Despite the rapid increase of world population, Christianity is simply growing faster than any other global religion when what is measured is its most relevant type of growth—the growth of committed adherents.

*Fig. 1. The number of evangelical Christians in the world compared to the number of non-Christians in the world over the course of human history. Neither category includes merely nominal Christians. But even in a worst-case scenario, where all the nominal Christians were included with the non-Christians as needing to be evangelized, there would still today be only about nine non-believers for every evangelical believer in the world. Undoubtedly, God's invisible Kingdom extends far beyond the boundaries of evangelicalism. (*Mission Frontier* magazine, November 1990, www.missionfrontier.org)*

in God's Kingdom is due in part to the presence of natural and moral evils in the world. It may well be the case that only in a world involving natural and moral evil that is gratuitous with respect to producing worldly happiness that the maximum number of people will freely come to know God and His salvation. To carry his argument,

Sinnott-Armstrong would have to show that it is feasible for God to create a world in which the same amount of the knowledge of God is achieved, but with less suffering. This is sheer speculation. *But so is his → argument...*

Doctrine #2: Mankind is in a state of rebellion against God and His purpose.

Rather than submit to and worship God, people rebel against God and go their own way, and so find themselves alienated from God, morally guilty before Him, and groping in spiritual darkness, pursuing false gods of their own making. The terrible human evils in the world are testimony to man's depravity in this state of spiritual alienation. The Christian is not surprised at the moral evil in the world; on the contrary, he *expects* it. The Bible says that God has given → *But* mankind over to the sin it has chosen; He does not intervene to stop *why is* it; He lets human depravity run its course. This only serves to heighten *their evil* mankind's moral responsibility before God, as well as our own *to begin* wickedness and our need of forgiveness and moral cleansing. *with?)*

Doctrine #3: God's purpose spills over into eternal life.

In the Christian view, this life is not all there is. Jesus promised eternal life to all who place their trust in him as their Savior and Lord. In the afterlife, God will reward those who have borne their suffering in courage and trust with an eternal life of unspeakable joy. The apostle Paul, who wrote much of the New Testament, lived a life of incredible suffering. Yet he wrote, "We do not lose heart. For this slight, momentary affliction is preparing us for an eternal weight of glory beyond all comparison, because we look not to the things that are seen, but to the things that are unseen, for the things that are seen are transient, but the things that are unseen are eternal" (II Corinthians 4.16–18). Paul imagines a scale, as it were, in which all the sufferings of this life are placed on one side, while on the other side is placed the glory that God will bestow on His children in heaven. The weight of glory is so great that it is literally beyond comparison with the suffering. Moreover, the longer we spend in eternity the more the sufferings of this life shrink by comparison toward an infinitesimal moment. That's why Paul could call them a "slight, momentary affliction"—they were simply overwhelmed by the ocean of divine eternity and joy that God lavishes on His children in heaven. Given the prospect of eternal life, we shouldn't expect to see in this life God's reasons for permitting every evil. Some may be justified only in light of eternity.

Given these three doctrines, we should expect much of the suffering in the world to appear gratuitous. In order to show that it really is gratuitous, Sinnott-Armstrong would have to refute these three doctrines, which he hasn't even tried to do.

3. *The most important factor in weighing whether the suffering in the world is really gratuitous will be—ironically—whether God exists!* That is to say, Sinnott-Armstrong's own argument shows that if God exists, then the suffering in the world is not gratuitous. Thus, we may argue:

1. If God exists, gratuitous suffering does not exist.
2°. God exists.
3°. Therefore, gratuitous suffering does not exist.

Thus, if God exists, then the apparently gratuitous suffering in the world is not really gratuitous.

So the issue comes down to which is true: (2) or (2°)? In order to prove that God does not exist, Sinnott-Armstrong would have to show that (2) is considerably more probable than (2°). As Daniel Howard-Snyder points out in his book *The Evidential Problem of Evil*, an argument from evil is a problem only for the theist "who finds all its premises and inferences compelling and who has lousy grounds for believing theism."[14] But if you have better reasons for believing that God exists, then, he says, evil "is not a problem."[15]

In response to what he calls the "Overriding Response," Sinnott-Armstrong again appeals to human analogies. He says that just because you had evidence that your neighbor was a good person, you wouldn't believe that you were hallucinating when you saw your neighbor beat his child. This analogy is flawed in two respects. First, it is unjustified to compare God's *permitting* harm and the neighbor's *perpetrating* harm. It is clearly emotionally prejudicial to put God in the role of the abusive neighbor. Second, God's having a morally sufficient reason for permitting evil is not analogous to your having a hallucination of your neighbor. (The hallucination analogy is more appropriate to a Hindu view that conceives of evil as part of *maya*, the realm of mere appearance.) Rather a better analogy would be if you lived next to the Sinnott-Armstrongs and one day you look next door and see Walter Sinnott-Armstrong standing there while someone else is beating his daughter, and he does nothing to help. Should you conclude, despite your previous evidence to the contrary, that Walter Sinnott-Armstrong is really an evil monster? Or wouldn't you suspect that Walter has a morally sufficient reason for allowing this to happen (for example, that there are intruders in his house and one of them has a gun to his wife's head and will shoot if Walter tries to stop the beating)? In the same way, if we have good evidence that God exists, then that increases the probability that He has a morally sufficient reason for permitting apparently gratuitous suffering. So you must balance the probability that apparently gratuitous suffering really is gratuitous against the probability that God exists. Even if, despite our cognitive limitations, we assign some positive probability to the former, the latter may still outweigh it.

Sinnott-Armstrong tries to block this route by saying that my arguments on behalf of theism do not prove that God is all-powerful and all-good. But my moral argument, if cogent, certainly does prove that God is all-good; and the cosmological argument certainly shows that the Creator of the universe out of nothing has sufficient power to prevent the evils that afflict our world, so that the success of my arguments *does* count against the gratuity of the suffering we observe. Moreover, my argument from the life, death, and resurrection of Jesus and my appeal to the proper basicality of belief in God go to support the existence of the biblical God, who is declared to be holy and almighty. In any case, Sinnott-Armstrong's atheism wouldn't be much of an atheism if it were consistent with the existence of a personal Creator and Designer of the universe, who is the locus of absolute value and who has revealed Himself in Jesus Christ and Christian experience! Remember, the problem of evil is supposed to be a positive argument for atheism.

In fact, far from being a positive argument for atheism, evil itself turns out, I believe, to be a positive argument for theism. For much of the suffering in the world is moral in nature; that is to say, the suffering inflicted by people on their innocent victims is genuinely evil. But then we may argue as follows:

1. If God does not exist, objective moral values do not exist.
2. Evil exists.

3. Therefore, objective moral values exist—namely, some things are evil!
4. Therefore, God exists.

Thus, evil paradoxically goes to prove God's existence, since without God things would not be good or evil as such. Notice that this argument thus shows the compatibility of God and evil without giving us a clue as to *why* God permits evil. We could be as ignorant of God's reasons as was Job in the Old Testament. But even in the absence of any answer to the "why" question, the present argument proves that evil does not call into question, but actually requires, God's existence. So although, superficially, evil seems to call into question God's existence, at a deeper level it actually proves God's existence, since without God, evil as such would not exist.

So, in summary, we've seen that Sinnott-Armstrong's attempt to prove the second premise of his argument:

2. Gratuitous suffering exists

is by no means successful.

But it should also be noted that his first premise:

1. If God exists, gratuitous suffering does not exist

itself is not obviously true. Some theists have suggested that while God could eliminate this or that specific instance of suffering without decreasing the goodness of the world, nevertheless there must exist a certain amount of gratuitous suffering in the world if the goodness of the world is not to be impaired. Thus the probability that a certain specified instance of suffering is gratuitous would not adversely affect theism. Indeed, it's not at all improbable that only in a world in which gratuitous natural and moral evils exist that the optimal number of persons would freely come to salvation and the knowledge of God. Sinnott-Armstrong might say that in that case the suffering is not really gratuitous after all: it serves the greater good of securing people's eternal salvation. But if one allows a greater good of *that* sort to count against the gratuity of suffering, then that makes it all the more difficult for one to prove that truly gratuitous suffering exists, for how could we possibly surmise what in God's providential plan for history does or does not contribute to the ultimate salvation of the greatest number of people?

In conclusion, the intellectual problem of evil—whether in its internal or external versions—can be satisfactorily solved, and so does not constitute a proof of atheism.

To wrap up, none of Sinnott-Armstrong's three arguments for atheism is, at the end of the day, rationally compelling or, at least, as rationally compelling as my five reasons in support of Christian theism. I, therefore, believe that the scales of the evidence tip in favor of theism rather than atheism.

Notes

1. The plausibility of the principle trades on the ambiguity of the word "evidence." If we mean that everything we believe must be inferentially derived by sound arguments from other beliefs, then contemporary epistemologists recognize that so stringent a demand would lead to skepticism, since even such obviously true beliefs as that *the external world exists* or that *the past is real* cannot be proven in this way. Rather such beliefs are properly basic beliefs not founded on argument. On the other hand, if we take "evidence" so broadly as to include the circumstances that ground properly basic beliefs, then it is not true that belief in God is not grounded by evidence. For a good discussion, see Alvin Plantinga, "Reason and Belief in God," in *Faith and Rationality*, ed. Alvin Plantinga and Nicholas Wolterstorff (Notre Dame, Ind.: University of Notre Dame Press, 1983), 16–93.

2. See the helpful booklet by Paul K. Moser, *Why Isn't God More Obvious?* (Atlanta: RZIM, 2000).

3. Alan G. Padgett, *God, Eternity, and the Nature of Time* (New York: St. Martin's Press, 1992), 33.

4. See my *Time and Eternity: Exploring God's Relationship to Time* (Wheaton, Ill.: Crossway, 2001), 86–109, as well as the discussion with Paul Helm, Alan Padgett, and Nicholas Wolterstorff in Gregory Ganssle, ed., *God and Time* (Downer's Grove, Ill.: Inter-Varsity Press, 2001).

5. He states this during our debate "Do Suffering and Evil Disprove God?" (April 2, 2000), Wooddale Church, Eden Prairie, Minn.

6. See pp. 5–6.

7. See further J. P. Moreland, "Libertarian Agency and the Craig/Grünbaum Debate about Theistic Explanation of the Initial Singularity," *American Catholic Philosophical Quarterly* 71 (1998): 539–554.

8. William Alston, "The Inductive Problem of Evil," *Philosophical Perspectives* 5 (1991): 65, 59.

9. This fact was already appreciated even in classical physics, as James Clerk Maxwell discerned:

"In all such cases there is one common circumstance—the system has a quantity of potential energy, which is capable of being transformed into motion, but which cannot begin to be so transformed till the system has reached a certain configuration, to attain which requires an expenditure of work, which in certain cases may be infinitesimally small, and in general bears no definite proportion to the energy developed in consequence thereof. For example, the rock loosed by frost and balanced on a singular point of the mountain-side, the little spark which kindles the great forest, the little word which sets the world a-fighting, the little scruple which prevents a man from doing his will, the little spore which blights all the potatoes, the little gemmule which makes us philosophers or idiots. Every existence above a certain rank has its singular points: the higher the rank, the more of them. At these points, influences whose physical magnitude is too small to be taken account of by a finite being, may produce results of the greatest importance."

(J. C. Maxwell, "Science and Free Will," quoted in L. Campbell and W. Garnett, *The Life of James Clerk Maxwell* [London: Macmillan, 1882], 443.)

10. Alston, "The Inductive Problem of Evil," p. 61.

11. David Martyn Lloyd-Jones, *From Fear to Faith; Studies in the Book of Habbakuk* (London: Inter-Varsity Fellowship, 1953), 23–24.

12. Patrick Johnstone, *Operation World* (Grand Rapids, Mich.: Zondervan, 1993), 164, 207–208, 214.

13. Ibid., p. 25.

14. Daniel Howard-Snyder, "Introduction," in *The Evidential Argument from Evil*, ed. Daniel Howard-Snyder (Bloomington: Indiana University Press, 1996), xi.

15. Ibid.

CHAPTER 6

Atheism Undaunted

Walter Sinnott-Armstrong

"You just don't get it," say some women to men who fail to understand their point of view. I feel like saying the same thing to Craig. He tries to respond to my three arguments, but sometimes he misses the point, and other times his reply leads him to a position that strikes me as desperate.

The Real Argument from Ignorance

Craig charges my argument from ignorance with a "subtle but crucial shift." (107) However, this criticism misrepresents my argument. Craig's point is that a certain principle—"we should not believe in entities for which we have no evidence"—"at best supports agnosticism, not atheism." (107) Of course, this principle *by itself* can't yield atheism! That's why my argument did not stop with this principle. Perhaps I was not clear enough, but the earlier passages in my section on "The Argument from Ignorance" were merely supposed to set the stage for my argument. After all, atheists need to agree with agnostics on one thing, namely, that we should not believe in God.

My argument for atheism comes later. When Craig does discuss my later argument, he accuses me of "a bizarre role reversal" in my discussion of gold on Uranus. (108) This discussion would have been bizarre if I had claimed that God was like gold on Uranus. But I never claimed anything like that. My point was to draw a crucial contrast between the issue of gold on Uranus and the issue of God's existence. The difference, as I tried to make clear, is that a lack of evidence for gold on Uranus would *not* show that we should believe that there is no gold on Uranus, whereas the lack of evidence for God *does* show that we should believe that there is no God. That is why I said that some arguments from ignorance are fallacious, but others are not.

This crucial difference is captured by a premise in my argument that Craig ignored until later in his discussion. With this premise added, my argument takes this form:

1. If there were an all-good and all-powerful God who could act in time, then we would have strong evidence for the existence of God.
2. We do not have strong evidence for the existence of God.
3. Hence, there is no all-good and all-powerful God who can act in time.

Background premise (1), which can be called *the strong evidence principle*, is what enables my argument to reach the conclusion of atheism and not just agnosticism. Its basic idea is simply that, if God existed, He would make it easier for us to know Him. God would not hide his light under a bushel, for the same reasons that Jesus tells his followers not to hide their lights under bushels. (Matthew 5:15–16) The point of the argument from ignorance is that God Himself does not follow Jesus' advice! He has a point...

The strong evidence principle is, admittedly, controversial. Some theists might deny it. That is why I argued for it. I listed many benefits of God revealing Himself more clearly to us. For example, believers would suffer less from doubt, and some potential criminals would be deterred by fear of divine punishment. I also argued against many commonly claimed costs of strong evidence for God, including supposed losses of faith and freedom. My point there was that the evidence for God could be *much* stronger than it is without undermining freedom or faith. These arguments showed that strong evidence for God would make our lives better overall, so an all-good, all-powerful God would give us strong evidence for God, just as the strong evidence principle claims.

Once premise (1) is established, all I need is premise (2). That premise was supported by my arguments in Chapter 2, which refuted the best evidence for God that Craig could produce in Chapter 1. As I write this chapter, I have not yet seen Craig's response in Chapter 3 to my criticisms in Chapter 2 of his arguments in Chapter 1; so I cannot yet respond to his response. But that, of course, does not mean that Craig has succeeded in defending his arguments against my criticisms. Indeed, even if Craig (or you) did find something wrong with the particular criticisms that I gave, that does not show that Craig's arguments do not fail in other ways or that his arguments provide strong evidence for a traditional God. If his arguments provide any evidence at all, it isn't strong.

One major flaw, as I have said, is that Craig's conclusions are badly bloated. Even if his arguments seem relevant to several (not all!) traditional features of God, all of his arguments together still cannot show that one single God has all of these features together. The creator of the universe (even if there were one) need not be the ground of moral value or the source of anyone's religious experiences today, much less the force that raised Jesus from the dead (even if this did happen). Craig cannot legitimately assume that all of his conclusions about various features apply to a single unified being. But he does assume this. This assumption is hidden when Craig formulates his arguments in terms of "God," since to refer to God in all of his arguments is to assume that there is a single being with all of these features. If Craig's conclusions instead referred to a creator, a ground of moral value, an external source of religious experience, and a Jesus-raiser, then it would be clear that these might be separate beings and that Craig has no reason to assume that these are all the same person (much less that the Christian Bible gives an accurate picture of that person). That conclusion goes far beyond anything that his arguments could establish even if they did work (which they do not). Moreover, this gap in his argument leads directly to the problem of ignorance: If there were an all-good and all-powerful God, He could, should, and would give us strong reason to believe that He exists as a single unified being. The fact that we have no strong evidence for a unified being with all of these features, thus shows that there is no such being.

Some readers still might be impressed by Craig's arguments that depend on recent scientific advances or historical scholarship. These references might seem sophisticated, but they feed right into my argument from ignorance. To see why, think back 200 years to times before those scientific theories were formulated, when nobody yet had heard of a Big Bang. People at those times could not use Craig's scientific arguments; so, even if those arguments do work today, those earlier people did not have any strong evidence for the existence of God. Thus, premise (2) was true *for them*. Premise (1) is also true for them, since any all-good God would care as much about them as about us, so He would reveal Himself to them. He would have no reason to let so many people in the past remain ignorant of Him for so long. Thus, premises that are only about those earlier people would be enough to reach my conclusion that there is no all-good and all-powerful God. Craig's appeals to recent science cannot solve this problem of ignorance.

It is still possible that other arguments, different from the ones that Craig gave, provide strong evidence that God exists. However, this is merely a possibility. Until we actually see much better arguments for the existence of God, there is reason to accept premise (2). With premises (1) and (2) in place, atheism follows.

Of course, Craig rejects both premises, but that does not show that those premises are flawed. In Chapter 5, at least, Craig has not given us any good reason to doubt either premise. He does call premise (1) "enormously presumptuous," and he asks, "why should [God] want to do such a thing?" (109) I already answered that question when I discussed the many benefits for humans of God revealing himself more clearly. So Craig's rhetorical question has no force at this point in our discussion.

Craig rejects my answer because, "in the Christian view, it is a matter of relative indifference to God whether people (merely) believe that He exists or not." (109) The point of his qualification "merely" seems to be that belief in God without love of God will not satisfy God: "what God is interested in is building a love relationship with you, not just getting you to believe that He exists."[1] (109) Fine, but God still should have *some* interest in mere belief, even if He *prefers* more than mere belief. One reason is that belief in God, even without love of God, has important benefits for humans. Imagine a contract killer who does not believe in God. Suppose that, if this contract killer did believe in God, then he would not love God, but he still would refrain from murder because he would fear punishment by God. This contract killer might be better off believing in God. Even if this killer did not benefit, this killer's potential victims would be better off if this killer believed in God. Thus, if God cares about the victims, then God has reason to make Himself more manifest to this killer and to other wrongdoers, regardless of whether they love Him.

Furthermore, even if mere belief is not sufficient to satisfy God, it is still necessary. You cannot have a love relationship with anything unless you believe that it exists. I can't love my sister if I don't know that I have a sister. Consequently, even if God does not want us "just" or "merely" to believe in Him, God still would want us to believe in Him, as a necessary condition for loving Him. This makes it hard to see any way around the conclusion that God cares about whether humans believe that God exists.

Here is where Craig's second response kicks in: "there is no reason at all to think that if God were to make His existence more manifest, more people would come into a saving relationship with Him." (109) No reason at all? Here's one: Those who now love and believe in God would not lose their faith or love for God if His existence were made more manifest in the proper way. Some others who do not now believe in God would come to believe in Him if His existence were more manifest. Not all of these new believers will love God, but some will, especially if God reveals His goodness. So there would be more people who believe in God and love God if His existence were more manifest.

The only way in which this argument could fail is if the new evidence made enough people lose their love for God. Craig talks about "a neon cross in the sky" and "brazen advertisements" that make people "chafe" and "resent such effrontery." (109) This parody misses my point. Such bungling is beneath God. Surely an all-knowing and all-powerful God could find and use some way to make Himself more manifest, at least to non-believers, without undermining believers' love for Him. God could appear to each person with just enough evidence of the right kind to convince that individual. Or, at least, God could provide rapists and murderers with enough evidence to dissuade them from their rampages. This evidence need not be seen by non-criminal believers, in which case the evidence for non-believers could not turn those believers against God. Moreover, even if God did give extra evidence to believers, possibly in order to relieve their doubts, this evidence could be limited to whatever is appropriate. An all-powerful God wouldn't need to be "brazen" in order to give people better evidence than they now have for His existence. If God gave additional evidence in some proper way, then "more people would come into a saving relationship with Him" (109), and humans would benefit in many ways at little or no cost to anyone. I might not be able to specify exactly how God would do this, but an all-knowing God could figure out *how* to do it, an all-powerful God *could* do it, and an all-good God *would* do it.

Thus, if there were an all-powerful and all-good God who could act in time, then we would have strong evidence for the existence of God. This is premise (1), which I called the strong evidence principle, so that premise is secure. As I said, premise (2) is supported by my series of arguments in Chapter 2. Together these premises imply atheism. Nothing that Craig has said undermines that argument from ignorance.

The Continuing Problem of Action

Craig does not question my argument that a timeless God cannot be causally active in the temporal world. Indeed, Craig supports it with citations to his own previous publications. This agreement might seem inconsequential, because Craig does not endorse the view of God as timeless. However, many traditional theologians throughout the centuries and even today hold that God is timeless. Since Craig agrees that my argument refutes that popular version of traditional theism, he must grant that my argument accomplishes a lot.

Of course, Craig does not grant this argument any force against his own view of God as existing within time. Craig sees his temporal view of God as compatible with traditional Christianity insofar as "the Bible leaves it open as to whether we are to understand divine eternity as timelessness (atemporality) or as everlasting duration (omnitemporality)." (110) But the Bible leaves it open only insofar as it includes passages on both sides of this issue. Craig cites Psalm 90.2 in favor of the view that God is everlasting. Then he cites Jude 25, which describes God as existing "before all time" (in a common translation). This phrase (if it makes sense) suggests timelessness. If these verses are taken literally, then the Bible is not neutral in the sense of being committed to *neither* view. Instead, the Bible seems committed to *both* of these incompatible views of God's relation to time. Moreover, Jude 25 seems committed to the very view that Craig takes to be refuted by "our" argument.

Still, Bible passages can always be reinterpreted, so I do not want to make too much of these verses. Nor does it matter much to me that the view of God as timeless has been and continues to be so popular. I mention these passages only to explain why I focused on that view of God in Chapter 4. What matters now is whether my argument can be extended to refute Craig's own view of God as everlasting or omnitemporal.

In Craig's view, as I understand it, God exists wholly, indivisibly, and equally at all times and, presumably, also at all spatial locations. In addition, God is intrinsically changeless, although God can change extrinsically insofar as God's relations to other things change when those other things change. To bring this conception of God down to earth, Craig draws an analogy to humans: "I, for example, exist equally, wholly, and indivisibly at every moment of my existence." (111) This analogy is misleading at best. Since my life is a series of events taking place over years, the whole of me does not exist at any one moment. Even at a single moment, I am divisible, not only because my body can be cut into parts, but also because my mind can divide its attention (so I can make plans about what to do after dinner while also feeling a headache, and my plans are separate from my headache). For such reasons, humans cannot provide a good model for Craig's God.

But let's imagine (if we can) for the sake of argument that humans do "exist equally, wholly, and indivisibly at every moment of . . . existence." There is still another crucial difference between humans and God. Humans change internally as well as externally, whereas Craig's God is not supposed to change internally at all. When I argued that timeless beings cannot cause changes in the temporal world, my reason was that timeless beings cannot change, and only changes can cause other changes. This argument clearly applies to any being that does not change, even if that being exists in time. So it applies to God if God does not change, whether or not God is temporal.

Of course, Craig admits that God does change externally, and Craig explains this notion by adding, "He changes in His relations with temporal things." (111) It is not clear what this means. It might seem that one example is that, as my son grows stronger, he gets closer to God's power, and God then changes by getting closer to my son's power. But that can't be the idea, because God is infinitely powerful, so my son cannot get closer to God's power, no matter how powerful my son becomes. Let's try again: If I drive south from Chicago to New Orleans, I move from north of Memphis to south of Memphis. So Memphis changes from south of me to north of me, even though Memphis never changes its location. But that also can't be the idea, because God is not supposed to have any particular spatial location as opposed to any other. One more try: If I believe that the president of the United States is in Washington when he isn't, and I still believe it when the president gets back to Washington, then my cognitive state can change from false belief to true belief, even though my mental state did not change in itself at all. But that can't be the idea, because God is supposed not to have any false beliefs. He is supposed to know everything in advance. There are many other models of "external change." I can't go through them all here. Nonetheless, my point is that, even if the notion of external change makes sense in our world, it is far from clear that it makes any sense when applied to God. External changes seem to be excluded by God's other traditional features.

More importantly, even if God does change externally in some way, this is not the kind of change that can cause effects in our world. It is hardly enough to part the Red Sea or cause all of the other miracles that are attributed to God. External changes surely cannot explain how God could create the world, since there was nothing external to God before the world was created, so then there could not have been any external change in God that would have caused the world to exist. Thus, even if God did change externally, such changes would not be enough to save many traditional claims about God.[2]

Freedom is also a red herring. Craig describes what he takes to be my view of freedom. (111) His description is inaccurate. I could explain why, but that tangent would be irrelevant,[3] because I could adopt any view of freedom that I want and still give my argument that an internally changeless God cannot cause changes. To bring up freedom is to skirt the issue.

Similarly for determinism. Craig says, "the reason Sinnott-Armstrong makes his claim is because he is a determinist." (111)

However, determinism has nothing to do with it. That's why I did not mention determinism when I gave my argument. I didn't need that assumption. My argument here would not be affected in the least if quantum mechanics convinced me that some events occur without any deterministic cause. Indeed, indeterministic quantum mechanics helps my case by providing a model of how a Big Bang could arise out of quantum soup. I discussed that issue in Chapter 2. The point here is just that, even if determinism were false, that would not begin to show that Craig's God could cause anything.

In order to explain how his God could cause changes, Craig admits that he must depend on a "wholly different" account of causation, which he and others call "agent causation." Craig is right that "Sinnott-Armstrong has said nothing to show that . . . agent causation does not exist." (112) Not yet, but now I'll say something: Craig never explains agent causation in his essay. This lack of explanation makes it hard to criticize his view, but Craig's idea seems to be that the cause of an act is the agent as a whole rather than any particular change in the agent.

If that's what agent causation is, why should we admit it? Craig gives only this reason for accepting agent causation: "I obviously cause certain events to occur when they do rather than earlier or later." (111) "Obviously"! Well, this is not obvious at all once one thinks about it a bit more deeply. Sure, in common language we say things like, "Minnesota Fats sank the eight ball." But that is just shorthand. We all know that it was not Minnesota Fats as a whole that sank the eight ball. (He didn't literally put everything he had into the shot. His whole body wasn't up on the table knocking the ball into the pocket.) That common knowledge makes it unnecessary to add obvious qualifications. However, when we are being more careful and explicit, we say that what sank the eight ball was Minnesota Fats's last shot (that is, his action of moving his arms so as to move the cue stick and knock the cue ball in a certain direction). In this and all other cases, it is not the agent as a whole who causes changes. The cause is, instead, a particular act by that agent at a particular time and place. The only reason why we do not mention this act in common language is that it is so obvious. The reason why it is obvious is that Minnesota Fats was in the pool hall all evening, but he did not sink the eight ball until midnight. His mere existence or presence cannot cause the event at midnight if he was there all night. It has to be some particular change at or before midnight that causes the event at midnight. So, if agent causation is causation by the agent as a whole, it makes no sense.[4]

Maybe Craig assumes a different notion of agent causation. Maybe this other notion makes sense. It is hard to tell until Craig explains what he means. Until then, agent causation remains mysterious and dubious at best. So the problem of action still gives another reason to believe that a traditional God does not exist.

The Unsolved Problem of Evil

My final argument, which Craig aptly labels "atheism's killer argument" (112), raises the classic problem of evil. When an argument is a "killer," opponents often simplify it in order to hide its force. So Craig reformulates my argument with two simple premises: "If God exists, gratuitous suffering does not exist. Gratuitous suffering exists. Therefore, God does not exist." (114) This common reformulation obscures several important points. First, my argument is not about suffering alone. Many forms of evil or harm do not involve suffering. Death and disability are evil or harmful to some extent, even when they are painless. Second, the term "gratuitous" is misleading, because the problem of evil arises even if evil is never *totally* gratuitous in the sense that there is no compensation at all for the evil. Atheists need to claim only that there is no *adequate* compensation for some cases of evil or harm. In response, theists cannot simply point to some small compensation. They need to argue that the compensation is adequate, which means that it must be not only important enough but also fair. Third, it is not enough that an evil is "ultimately to our or others' advantage," (114) as Craig says. To be justified, the evil must be *necessary* for that good. Otherwise, God could bring about the good without the evil. Finally, the argument targets only a traditional conception of God as all-powerful. Because God is supposed to be all-powerful, theists cannot argue simply that an evil brings about good in the world as we know it. Theists need to deny that there is any logically (or maybe metaphysically) possible world in which the good occurs without the evil or something else at least as bad. In response, atheists need to claim only that it is logically possible to gain the good without the evil, so atheists can refer to worlds that are very different, even in their basic laws of nature, from the world we live in. After all, an all-powerful God could have brought about those other possible worlds instead of ours.

For these reasons, I want to return to my original formulation:

1. If there were an all-powerful and all-good God, then there would not be any evil in the world unless that evil is logically necessary for an adequately compensating good.
2. There is lots of evil in the world.
3. Much of that evil is not logically necessary for any adequately compensating good.
4. Therefore, there is no God who is all-powerful and all-good.

Craig does not deny that this argument is logically valid. How could he? Nor does he deny premise (2). That one is obvious. He does raise some questions about premise (1) later (126).[5] However, Craig's main criticisms of my argument are directed at premise (3).

I supported premise (3) by citing numerous examples of harms and then ruling out a long list of goods that are often supposed to compensate for those evils. None of these arguments is absolutely conclusive. I already admitted that. But Craig uses (or abuses) my admission in his criticisms. So I need to start with a few words about the obscure, methodological issue of burden of proof.

Craig often suggests that my argument fails unless I prove premise (3) beyond any shadow of a doubt. Craig makes this assumption, for example, when he writes,

> A butterfly fluttering on a branch in West Africa may set in motion forces that would eventually result in a hurricane over the Atlantic Ocean. Yet it is impossible in principle for anyone observing that butterfly palpitating on a branch to predict such an outcome. The brutal murder of an innocent man or a child's dying of leukemia could send a ripple effect through history so that God's morally sufficient reason for permitting it might not emerge until centuries later or perhaps in another country. (117)

Notice the words "may," "could," "might," and "perhaps." Similar guarding terms occur again and again throughout Craig's Chapter 5.[6] Such qualifications take the sting out of Craig's response. Sure, a butterfly *might* cause a hurricane. I can't exclude that possibility.

Nonetheless, when I see a butterfly fluttering, I have no reason at all to believe that *this* butterfly will *actually* cause a hurricane. Similarly, it is possible that a child's dying of leukemia would stop all of the fighting in the Middle East. Nonetheless, when I see a child dying of leukemia, I have no reason at all to believe that *this* child's death will *actually* prevent any war.

What does this show about my premise (3)? In any example that I give to support premise (3), I must admit the possibility that the cited evil is necessary for some adequately compensating good. (It's not clear how this necessity could be logical, but I will let that go for now.) So it is possible that this example does not really support premise (3). Still, all that I have to admit is a possibility. Despite this possibility, in each of my examples, we have no *reason* to believe that the cited evil is *actually* necessary for some adequately compensating good.

Now apply this point to the range of examples. There are many cases of many kinds where we have no reason, even after careful reflection, to believe that an evil is necessary for any adequately compensating good. It is possible that all of these evils are justified in ways that we cannot see, just as it is possible that every fluttering butterfly causes a hurricane. But to admit that this is *possible* is not to admit that it is true or even *plausible*. Surely we have plenty of reason to believe that much evil out of this vast set is not logically necessary for any adequately compensating good. That is all that premise (3) claims. So we have plenty of reason to believe premise (3).

Is that enough for my argument? Not if each premise must be proven beyond a shadow of a doubt, as Craig seems to assume. However, that burden of proof is too heavy to be met on any important and controversial matter. We could not live our lives well if we never took any risk of being wrong. We need to rely on fallible reasons. So it is enough that we do have plenty of reasons to accept premise (3).

The same point applies to another of Craig's complaints. He sometimes adds that we cannot "assess with confidence the probability that" (116) my premises are true. I admit that I cannot assign any definite probability between 0 and 1 to my premises. However, I also cannot assign a definite probability to many things I believe, such as that the butterfly fluttering in front of me now will not cause a hurricane. This limitation does not make my beliefs unreasonable.

If we had to assign definite probabilities to every belief, then we could not believe much, if anything, of importance in everyday life. As before, Craig's criticism depends on a very high standard that my belief does fail, but which need not be met in order for beliefs to be justified.

In other places, Craig suggests a different issue regarding burden of proof. He assumes that I need to show that Christians as such have reasons to accept my premises, so it is not enough to show that other people who are not Christians have such reasons. This assumption comes out, for example, when Craig replies, "the Christian is not committed by his world view to the truth of" (114) premise (3). The suggestion seems to be that my argument begs the question by invoking premises to which Christians are not committed.

Well, that depends on my goal and my audience. If I were trying to persuade Christians who immediately reject anything that is incompatible with their prior religious beliefs, then my task would be hopeless. So I am not trying to persuade such dogmatic Christians. This is *not* to admit that my arguments have no force against them. My arguments show that all traditional theists have adequate reasons to renounce their belief in God, so they should renounce that belief, even if they are not persuaded by those reasons, because they do not listen to my arguments. Religious beliefs lead many (not all!) people to refuse to listen to reasons, but that does *not* mean that those reasons lack force as reasons. All it means is that those people cannot be persuaded. But, as I said, my goal is not to persuade them. Nor is my argument aimed at atheists who immediately reject anything that is religious without caring about whether they have adequate reasons to do so. They don't need any argument from me or anyone else. Instead, my intended audience includes only those whose minds are open, that is, who are willing to consider evidence against the existence of God as well as for the existence of God and to form their beliefs on the basis of that evidence.

Most Christians whom I know fall into this category. However, Craig seems to assume that a Christian will reject any premise to which he is "not committed by his world view." What is this "world view?" If their world view as Christians includes only the essential doctrines of Christianity and the logical implications of those doctrines, then Christians are not committed to my premise (3) on that basis. However, Christians are not just Christians. They are also humans with common sense, so they hold many beliefs, as well as standards of adequate compensation, that are not essential doctrines of Christianity. These other views do commit most (even if not all) Christians to my premises.

Craig mentions one of these commonsense beliefs: "Everybody admits that the world is filled with *apparently* gratuitous suffering." (114) Craig emphasizes, "that doesn't imply that these apparently gratuitous evils really *are* gratuitous." (114) This statement is accurate if all it denies is a formal logical implication. Nonetheless, appearances still do affect the burden of proof. If a stick looks bent, then it is reasonable to think that it is bent, as long as there is no reason that overrides or undermines the visual appearance. If the stick also feels straight, or if a magician is waving it, then I should not trust my eyes. But if I feel it, look at it closely from all angles in various circumstances, and find no reason to doubt its bent appearance, then I have reason to believe that it is bent. Its bent appearance still doesn't "imply" that it is really bent, but no mere experience could logically imply that. We need to draw conclusions from how things appear to us, at least after close inspection.

Sticks are concrete (in one sense!), but the same method applies to less tangible topics. Would it benefit my family in the long run if I were to burn down our house tonight? Possibly. Does that possibility make it reasonable to believe that we would benefit? No. Why not? Because we do know one thing: Burning down my house would cause serious problems for my family in the short term. Those known costs set up a presumption or burden of proof that needs to be overcome before contrary beliefs can be reasonable. Given those known costs, if I have no reason to believe that burning down my house will bring adequate benefits, then it is *not* reasonable for me to believe that burning down my house will benefit my family overall in the long term. Moreover, it is reasonable for me to believe that burning down our house will *not* benefit us overall in the long term. Don't you agree? If so, we both seem committed to some standard like this: When something causes serious short-term costs, and we have no reason to believe that it is necessary for any adequate compensation in either the short term or the long term, then it is not reasonable to believe that it is good overall in the long term, and it is reasonable to believe that it is not good overall in the long term. Most theists are committed to that commonsense standard, even though it does not follow from any essential Christian doctrine. They have reason to accept it, because without it they would be lost in their everyday lives. They might end up burning down their houses!

Craig seems to think that this standard is undermined by my claim that "we have no more reason to believe that the evil now will lead to great bliss in the long term than that this evil will lead to great misery." (118) However, my point was that, without any reason to believe that either long-term effect is more likely than the other, possible long-term benefits are canceled by possible long-term costs. But short-term consequences are another matter. We can still know a lot about the evil now and its short-term costs, at least in the cases that I was discussing. What is known about these evils then sets up a presumption that is not rebutted by any other reasons. That is why my admission of ignorance about long-term effects supports my argument rather than undermines it in the way that Craig suggests.

This commonsense standard leads right into my argument. We know that evil occurs, as premise (2) says. The existence of that evil sets up a presumption. This presumption is never overcome, because we have no reason to believe that this evil is logically necessary for any adequate compensation in either the short term or the long term. I supported this premise by ruling out the many proposed justifications of evil. The presumption plus the absence of any rebuttal makes it reasonable to believe that the evil is not good overall. That, in turn, makes it reasonable to believe that there is no all-good and all-powerful God.

So far I have focused on standards for when beliefs are reasonable, but my arguments against proposed justifications of evil also employ a different kind of standard, namely, standards for when compensation is adequate. Here again I claim that my standards are commonsense principles that most Christians accept, along with almost everyone else.

For example, Craig suggests that God's reason for allowing babies to suffer and die might be a combination of heaven and virtue: The babies go to heaven, and other people develop moral virtue. In Chapter 4, I pointed out that an all-powerful God could send the babies straight to heaven without the evil, but Craig responds, "that forgets the Virtuous Response: so doing would short-circuit God's work in the lives of the parents or other people." (116) I didn't forget that. Rather, I assumed that gains to other people would not be adequate compensation for harm to the baby, for reasons that I gave in my very next section on the Virtuous Response. One reason is that an all-powerful God would have at His disposal less harmful ways to teach lessons. Another reason is that it would be unfair to let the baby suffer just to help separate individuals. Here I was appealing to a commonsense standard of adequate compensation, namely, that it is morally wrong to use some people merely as means to benefit other people, at least when one could benefit those other people in a less harmful way. This standard would be accepted by consequentialists, by Kantians, and also by defenders of the natural law doctrine of double effect (since, in the relevant case, God would intend harm as a means, thereby violating this doctrine). This standard is not completely clear, but surely one example is letting a baby die painfully merely to teach a moral lesson to other people, when one has less harmful ways to teach those other people. Any human who did this would be considered a moral monster, so the same compensation also should not count as adequate for God.

Craig complains about my analogies, so I should explain why I use them. I admit that analogies are dangerous. One reason is that opponents can always find some disanalogy. No analogy is perfect. But, also, not every difference matters. The analogy still works if the differences that do exist do not matter. So analogies can be useful when theists would simply deny any direct claim about God. If theists admit the analogous case, their admission reveals their commitment to a general principle, and then the burden is on them to explain why that general principle does not apply to God. That is the strategy behind my analogies. I am trying to show that common sense commits you to the premises of my argument. If you agree with me about my everyday examples, that admission reveals your own standards for reasonable belief or adequate compensation. My argument simply applies those same standards to belief in God.

Craig suggests that Christians might deny that such common standards apply to God: "I am bound by certain moral obligations and prohibitions vis à vis my neighbor (e.g., not to take his life); but God (if He has moral duties at all) is not bound by many of these (e.g.

He can give and take life as He pleases)." (115) Of course, if God is all-powerful, then God is *able* (in the sense of having the power) to "take life as He pleases." However, that ability shows nothing about "*moral* obligations and prohibitions." So I take Craig's final parenthetical claim to be that there is nothing morally wrong with God killing anyone at any time for any reason, no matter how trivial the reason is. In this view, people have no more rights than mosquitoes with respect to God. Why not? Maybe because God is so powerful. But might does not make right. Maybe because God created us. But parents are prohibited from killing the children whom they create and nurture. Why? Because the children are separate people with rights. This reason applies to God as well. If God gave us free will, then He made us separate people, so why wouldn't we have rights not to be killed by Him needlessly? I see no good reason to exempt God from moral standards, so I assume that He would not be justified in letting babies suffer and die merely as a means to benefit other people when he has better alternatives.

If Craig continues to insist that God is morally permitted to "take life as He pleases," then his obstinacy will strike many people as desperate. Most Christians will hope for a better response. After all, God is supposed to be all-good. Craig's response admits that God violates the only moral standards that we know. If God's goodness is compatible with letting babies die painfully merely as a means to help other people when God could use less harmful means to help those other people, then this is a kind of goodness that we do not understand or have any reason to care about. Why should we love or worship a God who does such things? It might sound neat to say that God is not subject to our standards, but this ploy leaves it unclear what it is that makes God good. In the end, we need to use our own standards, because we cannot understand any others.

Luckily, Craig gives other responses. Sometimes he argues that all evil can be justified in terms of common moral standards. What a theist needs is for each bit of evil to be justified by something. Theists do not need a single justification to cover all bits of evil. They can use different justifications for different bits of evil, as long as every bit ends up being justified. Craig accuses me of forgetting this logical point by adopting a "divide and conquer" strategy. I plead innocent. I did not "typically refute . . . a solution by arguing that it cannot cover *all* cases of suffering," (115) as Craig charges. Instead, I gave several examples, such as birth defects, and argued that no proposed compensation, either alone or in combination with others, is adequate to justify the evil in those specific cases. Even if "the solutions are complementary and mutually reinforcing" (116) *when* they apply, that does not show that they *do* apply to the cases in my argument. Besides, I argued (four paragraphs back) that the solutions do *not* mutually reinforce each other in the way that Craig claims, at least in the examples that I gave. So, far from "divide and conquer," my strategy was to focus my forces in a few examples that undermine all proposed justifications together.

Later in Chapter 5, Craig does propose one justification that might seem to solve the problem of evil, if it worked. He claims that "the purpose of life is . . . knowing God," (120) and "it is precisely in countries that have endured severe hardship that evangelical Christianity is growing at its greatest rates." (121) This is supposed to show that severe hardship serves the purpose of life.

The first problem here is that Craig's factual claim is dubious at best. He cites Johnstone on China as one example. (121) Reportedly, harsh persecution of Christians during Mao's Cultural Revolution was followed by unparalleled growth in the number of Christians. This report should come as no surprise, because it must be based on what people communicated about their beliefs. The number of people who are willing to publicly proclaim their Christianity is likely to go down while Christians are persecuted harshly, even if the number of believers does not go down. Anyway, let's grant for now that the number of Christians did go way down under Mao, because of fear and inability to obtain information about Christianity. That low point would explain why many people in China did become Christians when information became available and fear was removed. But the number of Christians is still probably less than what it would have been if there had been no persecution in the first place. That comparison is the relevant measure of whether the evil of persecution led to more knowledge of God. So neither Craig nor Johnstone is justified in calling Mao "the greatest evangelist in history." (121)

Most importantly, even if Mao's policies did increase the number of Christians, Craig himself says, "It is estimated that 20 million Chinese lost their lives during Mao's Cultural Revolution." (121) To glorify such a tragedy dishonors the memory of the victims. Surely an omnipotent God could find a less costly way to produce Christians in China.

Craig also mentions El Salvador and Ethiopia. I will not discuss those cases here because similar points apply. Even if the number of Christians does go up after tragedies, there is no reason to think that an all-powerful God could not find a less harmful way to help people come to know and love Him.

Besides, if every such tragedy really were necessary for a higher purpose, then we ought to welcome tragedies and not fight them. We should let Mao persecute the Chinese, and let earthquakes destroy lives in El Salvador, and let famines ravage Ethiopia, and so on. If all such tragedies were God's plan, to interfere in any of them would be to interfere in God's plan and to prevent the greater good of more people becoming Christian. Luckily, not all Christians hold such beliefs. Many Christians work hard against evils in this world. But Craig suggests a different view of tragedies when he says that so many deaths and so much suffering are a "slight, momentary affliction" that "only serves to heighten mankind's moral responsibility before God." (123) Such a view takes away our incentive to help each other in this world. Beliefs with this result should be avoided, at least in the absence of any reason to accept them. And nothing that Craig says gives us any reason to accept such a view or to believe that tragedies like those in China, El Salvador, and Ethiopia really do cause growth in evangelical Christianity or serve any worthwhile purpose.

Although Craig fails to specify why God allows evil, he has one move left. He claims that his arguments for the existence of God show that God must have *some* reason to allow evil, even if we cannot figure out what it is. The conclusion that God has some unknown reason is supposed to follow from Craig's arguments for the existence of God.

Unfortunately, this move is no better than his arguments for the existence of God. I already argued at length in Chapter 2 that Craig's arguments for God fail miserably. I have seen no reason to take any of that back. Later, in Chapter 5, Craig merely repeats his claims that "my moral argument, if cogent, certainly does prove that God is all-good; and the cosmological argument certainly shows that the

Creator of the universe out of nothing has sufficient power to prevent the evils that afflict our world." (125) Again, Craig merely assumes without any argument that the "God" who is all-good is the same person as the creator. That assumption begs the question here, since the existence of evil is compatible with one being who is all-good and another separate being who is all-powerful. Besides, even if the moral argument were cogent evidence for some personal source of objective value (which it is not), it still would not "certainly . . . prove" that this source is *all*-good, since this source might fail its own objective standards of goodness. Regarding his claims for his cosmological argument, notice that Craig's use of the assuring term "certainly" is again misleading, since it is not at all certain that something powerful enough to create the whole universe around fifteen billion years ago was ever *all*-powerful, is still alive *today*, or is able to prevent every specific occurrence of evil. Many things that are powerful on a large scale (such as a supernova or the Big Bang) do not last forever and are as clumsy as a bull in a china shop when it comes to small details. Similarly, it might not be within a creator's abilities or job description to fix genetic defects in suffering children.

Of course, *if* a traditional God did exist, then, by definition, He would have "sufficient power to prevent the evils that afflict our world." But that would hardly show that God *does* exist. Indeed, God's supposedly unlimited power is exactly what creates the problem of evil and, thereby, demonstrates that God does *not* exist. Craig's arguments for the existence of God need to be much better than these in order to give us adequate reason to believe that all evil is justified in ways that we cannot see.

Craig does formulate one new argument when he claims that "evil . . . requires God's existence" because "If God does not exist, objective moral values do not exist." (125–126) This premise is, however, a strange way to begin an argument at this point in our book, because I already showed in Chapter 2 why that premise is dubious at best. Rape is morally wrong because it harms the victim, even if there is no God; so objective moral values can and do exist without God. Moreover, atheists can consistently and justifiably believe in moral values as much as theists can. Just consider all of the nonreligious moral theories that philosophers develop.

Where does all of this leave us? Craig is not convinced by my arguments. Nor am I convinced by his. That impasse should not surprise anyone. The more important question is whether our arguments provide reasons for open-minded inquirers who are not previously committed either for or against the existence of God.

Craig's arguments constantly depend on a prior belief in God. How else could he hold that a child's dying of leukemia and Mao's Cultural Revolution were good? How else could he start arguments with phrases like "Once we reflect on God's providence . . . "? (119) How else could he think that the problem of evil could be solved by Christian doctrines like "The purpose of life is . . . knowing God" (120) and "God's purpose spills over into eternal life"? (123) None of these claims has any force for anyone who is not already committed to the existence of God.

In contrast, I tried to base my arguments on commonsense standards of reasonable belief and adequate compensation. These principles are not peculiar to atheists. Most Christians also use the same standards in their everyday lives. More importantly, these principles are accepted by almost everyone who is not committed in advance either for or against the existence of God. That makes them neutral starting points.

Of course, when you put these principles together with obvious facts, they yield the conclusion that God does not exist. Otherwise my argument could not work. But that is no problem for my argument. Every argument has to start from premises that lead to its conclusion. The strategy in a good argument is to start from premises that are independent of the conclusion in the sense that the premises would and should be accepted by people who are not already committed one way or the other about the conclusion. My premises pass this test. Craig's do not. That is why I conclude that my arguments provide better reasons to believe that God does not exist.

Notes

1. Craig's guarding term "just" is misleading, because neither I nor anyone else believes that *all* God cares about is "getting you to believe that He exists." Any all-good God would care about many things other than belief in Him. But that does not mean that belief in God is not one of the things that God would care about, at least instrumentally as a means to other goods.

2. For more arguments that external (or Cambridge) changes cannot cause effects, see Sections I–II of Sydney Shoemaker, "Causality and Properties," in his *Identity, Cause, and Mind* (Cambridge: Cambridge University Press, 1984), 206–209.

3. At several points Craig says that I adopt or assume a view that I do not hold and that my argument does not depend on. When the ascribed view is implausible or absurd, this common rhetorical trick might lead some readers to distrust anyone who would hold such a view. That danger makes it tempting to respond to each charge, but then I would not have space for more important issues. For that reason, I will restrain myself and not bother to respond to each accusation. My silence should not be misconstrued as an admission of Craig's claims.

4. My brief argument against agent causation derives from C. D. Broad, "Determinism, Indeterminism, and Libertarianism," in his *Ethics and the History of Philosophy* (London: Routledge, 1952), 195–217. For more arguments, see Alvin Goldman, *A Theory of Human Action* (Princeton, N.J.: Princeton University Press, 1970), 80–85; and Hilary Bok, *Freedom and Responsibility* (Princeton, N.J.: Princeton University Press, 1988), 44 ff.

5. There, Craig says that premise (1) "is not obviously true" and has been questioned by "[s]ome theists." (126) Since he uses the third person, he does not seem to share these theists' views. In any case, Craig says how I would respond to those theists. His only criticism of my response brings the issue back to premise (3). That is why I focus only on premise (3) in my text.

6. Here are a few examples: "the envisioned revelation might lead to self-stultifying situations." (119) Maybe, but couldn't an all-powerful God avoid this problem? "Many evils occur in life that are utterly gratuitous with respect to the goal of producing human happiness; but they may not be gratuitous with respect to producing a deeper knowledge of God." (120) Or they may be gratuitous in that respect *as well*. The question is not what "might" or "may" be, but what we have adequate reason to believe

INDEX

A

Ackerman, Susan, 51 n. 2, 56

action, problem of, 61, 98–101, 110–112, 134–138

Acts, 110

actual infinite. *See* infinite, actual *vs.* potential

Adam, 90

Adams, Robert M., 68, 77 n. 22

advertisements for God, 109, 133

agnosticism, 81, 107–108, 129

Alston, William, 27, 68, 77 n. 22, 116, 119

analogies, 12, 16, 38, 39, 44, 46, 47, 48, 89, 90, 92, 96, 98, 100, 104, 114–115, 117, 124–125, 135, 144

argument from ignorance. *See* ignorance, argument from

atheism, 3, 81, 107–108, 129

atheistic moral realism, 19–20, 34, 67

B

Barrow, John, 15, 60

beg(ging) the question, 7, 48–49, 58, 96, 141, 148

Ben and Jerry, 38

Big Bang, 4–5, 9, 32, 43–45, 49, 60–61, 64, 132, 148

Big Crunch, 61

bloated conclusions, fallacy of, 32, 50, 53–54, 131

Bohm, David, 6

Boltzmann, Ludwig, 14–15, 66

Brandenburger, Robert, 13

Buddhists, 82

burden of proof, 139–145

C

Carr, B. J., 64

causation, 5, 8, 45, 100–101
    agent causation, 111–112, 137–138, 150 n. 4
    whatever begins to exist has a cause, 8–9, 56

chance, 10–11, 49, 64–67

change, external or extrinsic, 111, 135–136, 150 n. 2

chaos theory, 117, 139

Chaotic Inflationary Universe theory, 8, 13, 117

Collins, Robin, 63–66

common sense, 142–144, 149

Copenhagen Interpretation, 6, 56–57

Corinthians, 123

F

fallacies. *See* begging the
question; bloated
conclusions; equivocation;
excessive footnotes; false
dichotomy; genetic;
ignorance, argument
from; inverse gambler's;
straw man
false dichotomy, fallacy of, 32,
54–55
familiarity, 66
fine-tuning argument, 9–17,
46–50, 52 n. 13, 62–67
France, R. T., 55
free will (and freedom), 34, 68,
90, 92–93, 111, 117,
136–137, 145

G

Genesis, 110
genetic fallacy, 20
Gert, Bernard, 86
ghosts, 103
God
all-good, 31, 83–86, 97–98,
105, 112–114, 125, 134,
138–139, 145, 147–148
all-knowing (omniscient), 31,
83, 117, 133–134
all-powerful (omnipotent),
31, 51, 83–85, 97–98, 105,
112–114, 117, 119, 125,
133–134, 138–139,
147–148
changeless, 5, 54, 99, 135–136
effective (active in time), 31,
83, 98, 101

eternal and timeless, 5, 8,
31, 46, 83, 98–101,
110–111, 134–138
gender, 51n. 1
immaterial, 5, 54, 98
personal, 5–6, 31, 45–46, 54,
61, 83, 111
temporal, 61, 99–100,
110–111, 134–138
transcendent, 8
uncaused, 5, 54
unity, 131, 148
Gödel, Kurt, 42
Grand Unified Theories,
76 n. 10
Grass, Hans, 71
Great Pumpkin, 102

H

Hawking, Stephen, 8, 9, 32,
43–44, 55, 75 n. 9
Healey, John, 18, 32
Hengel, Martin, 71
Hick, John, 26, 32
Hilbert, David, 4, 32, 42,
75 n. 8
Hindus, 74, 82, 124
holocaust, 17
Howard-Snyder, Daniel, 124
Hoyle, Fred, 4, 32
Hume, David, 5, 32, 73

I

ignorance, argument from, 96,
101–105, 107–110,
129–134
as sometimes fallacious, 104,
130